Gutsy WOMEN

TRAVEL
TIPS
and
WISDOM
for the
ROAD

Gutsy WOMEN

TRAVEL
TIPS
and
WISDOM
for the
ROAD

BY MARYBETH BOND

Travelers' Tales, Inc.
San Francisco, California

Distributed by
O'Reilly and Associates
101 Morris Street, Sebastopol, CA 95472

Gutsy Women: Travel Tips and Wisdom for the Road
By Marybeth Bond

Cover design by Kathryn Heflin
Interior design by Susan Bailey
Cover photographs:
    Marybeth Bond in the Himalayas © Janet Fullwood, 1994
    Carmen Miranda © Wild Women Adventures, 1995
    Woman mountain biking © Brian Bailey, Tony Stone Images 1996
    Amelia Earhart in her flight suit, Nov. 1928
      © The National Archives/Corbis
    Two women in Antarctica, (organized by Overseas Adventure
      Travel for mature travelers) © Peter Smith, 1994

Printing History

October 1996:	First Edition
February 1997:	Second Printing
May 1997:	Third Printing

For my parents, Ruth and Bill Bond, and my husband Gary,
for urging me to fulfill my wildest dreams.

ISBN: 1-885211-15-5

$\mathscr{T}$ABLE OF $\mathscr{C}$ONTENTS

$\mathcal{I}$ NTRODUCTION

Travel not only stirs the blood...it also gives birth to the spirit.
—*Alexandra David-Neel, French explorer, writer*

———

SOMEONE RECENTLY TOLD ME we live our lives one of three ways: treadmill, saga, or pilgrimage. Take your pick, she said, for it is a choice you must make every day.

To avoid a saga in my own life and to get off the treadmill, I often feel compelled to hit the road. I create pilgrimages for myself, from an afternoon hike to an overnight trip, to an extended journey anywhere outside my zip code.

Am I frightened to travel? It depends. When I go on an organized tour—never! When I am free-wheeling with my husband—rarely. When I travel alone with my children—sometimes. And when I go solo—always! Then why bother?

Fear and discomfort about traveling diminishes with time and experience. Taking one small risk leads to taking larger risks until you realize you have made leaps of confidence and you are a competent and confident traveler. And more women are taking that first step every day.

Women now represent 44 percent of business travelers and it is estimated that in less than four years they will represent more than 50 percent. In 1996, 64 percent of adventure travelers were female. Women are responsible for more than 70 percent of the travel decisions for all types of travel and are spending more and more of their discretionary income on travel. Everyone is waking up to women's buying power and realizing that more and more women of all ages are taking to the road.

After publication of my book, *Travelers' Tales: A Woman's World*, I traveled nationwide on a book tour, and avid travelers and would-be travelers asked me hundreds of questions. From college students hitting the road for the first time to mature widows just beginning to spread their wings, women of all ages and levels of experience asked me for advice. Seasoned travelers in the audience shared their tried-and-true tips too.

Men, especially talk-show hosts, focused on the safety issue: "Weren't you concerned for your safety? Isn't travel risky? What about rape? What was your worst experience? Where would you recommend women *not travel*?"

Women more often asked: "How do you handle your money? How do you pack lightly? How do you handle eating alone in a restaurant? Are there countries women traveling alone should avoid? What are your tips for meeting people? How do you arrange visits in local homes and schools? What do you do on bad hair days, when you've been in remote areas and unable to bathe? Did you get sick? What's the best preventive medicine? Is there anywhere you can't buy tampons? What about condoms?"

This book is an attempt to answer these questions, to open doors for the novice, or to share advice across generations, among peers. *Gutsy Women* is a book of travel tips and wisdom but, like its predecessor, *A Woman's World*, it is about more than just travel. It is about living, the rewards of risk-taking, feeling, learning, loving, about the strength to be ourselves, to take steps toward making our dreams real.

Women are unique in many ways—in our view of the world, in our approach to life, in our expression of freedom. Relationships are important to us and we make connections quickly and easily. We also have unique concerns and issues. The moment we step out the door, we are aware of the footsteps behind us. We are concerned for our personal safety, and with good reason.

Is travel a risky business? Yes, but all of life is risky. We live in an unsafe country. And yet we have learned to cope and take care of ourselves in this environment. Following these same instincts in foreign countries will protect us.

By age twenty-nine I had already lived and traveled overseas for six years, but my appetite for travel was not satisfied, so I made preparations to take off and travel alone around the world. "You have good sense Marybeth, please use it," my mother urged me. She also asked that I promise not to take any drugs that would cloud my ability to make wise decisions. My father asked me to promise that I would carry enough money on me at all times to take a taxi, even a few blocks, to avoid dangerous situations after dark. I followed their advice.

Considering how much I have traveled over the past three decades—from Kathmandu to Killarney, from Ecuador to Tanzania—and considering I have often traveled alone and stayed in very modest accommodations, I have had very few threatening experiences. I have asked for help when I needed it; I've followed my instincts and the advice of seasoned travelers and have had remarkable adventures.

In the pages that follow you'll encounter words of wisdom from a multitude of experienced women travelers that will help you on your way, confirm your own instincts, or inspire new ideas about traveling in our world. At the back of the book are resources that will help answer your more specific questions, and a reading list to enhance your preparation.

Many gutsy women are already traveling, are on the road as you read this. And many more need only a word or two of encouragement to step out the door. Remember, you only need three things to have a great trip: your passport, your money, and above all, your sense of humor. *Bon voyage*.

I
$\mathscr{T}$HE $\mathscr{F}$IRST $\mathscr{S}$TEP

Life is like a mask dancing;
to see it well, you do not stand in one place.
—*African Proverb*

BEFORE WE DO ANYTHING IN LIFE, even the most impulsive of us do some preparation. We educate ourselves to prepare for careers, plan strategies for important meetings, make menus for simple or extravagant meals. Preparation helps us reduce fears by giving us knowledge and builds confidence by increasing our comfort with the unknown.

Preparing yourself mentally and emotionally for traveling overseas is just as important as getting your visas and shots. Give yourself time to work through fears you may have about safety, traveling alone, or fitting into a different culture. To convert your apprehension into excitement, begin your mental preparation weeks or even months prior to departure. Contact women who have gone before you. They will be your role models. You may connect with them by phone, via e-mail, or by reading their stories in travel books.

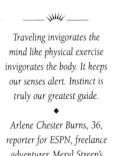

Traveling invigorates the mind like physical exercise invigorates the body. It keeps our senses alert. Instinct is truly our greatest guide.

♦

Arlene Chester Burns, 36, reporter for ESPN, freelance adventurer, Meryl Streep's coach, trainer, and stunt double for The River Wild, *Mosier, Oregon*

We discover the world as we physically move around the planet; we discover ourselves on the inner journey that accompanies our travels. The rewards are many: we try on new identities as more independent, self-sufficient women; we explore new behaviors; and we develop a greater awareness of our potential. Remind yourself that the minimal

The trick is not to rid your stomach of butterflies, but to make them fly in formation.

◆

Pacific Crest Outward Bound School, Book of Readings

risk of traveling is far outweighed by the rewards.

TIPS

➢ Do your research as far in advance as possible. Begin at your public library. Search by subject matter or country name through the computer for a listing of all magazine and newspaper articles, historical and political studies, novels, documentaries, and movies.

➢ Put travel anthologies on your reading list, including books by and about women and books that focus on the countries you want to visit. The Travelers' Tales series is a superb place to start.

➢ Seek out people who have traveled or lived in

Most people think they have too many responsibilities to travel, especially in the way that appeals to their fantasies. The hungry spouse, children, job, mortgage, school, army, or mother needs them. This is bullshit, of course. Most people are simply too afraid to step out of the rut to do something they would like to do. Honest, folks: the world doesn't end when you decide to do what you want to do, it merely begins.

◆

Ed Buryn, Vagabonding in Europe and North Africa

the country you'll be visiting and ask them lots of questions, especially about good reading material and if they know citizens from there who are living in the U.S.

➤ Contact your local university to see if there are foreign students from the country you will be visiting who would be willing to meet with you.

➤ Get on the Internet and browse through the travel chatrooms and especially the news groups. You may make interesting contacts with people from the country where you plan to travel. Often when you arrive you'll have a name and phone number of someone to look up.

➤ The local embassy or consulate can provide answers to general questions and will provide reading material upon request.

➤ Consider doing some volunteer work as part of your travels. Getting involved in volunteer organizations offers a great opportunity to deepen your experience and helps you get beneath the surface of a culture.

➢ Learn a few words in the local language— hello, good-bye, please, thank you, beautiful. If you have the time, take a language course.

➢ Get to know a good travel agent. You will never regret it, no matter how adept you become at your own trip planning.

> ___ ⟋⟋⟍⟍ ___
>
> *I never regretted any trip I took, no matter how inconvenient, expensive, or unnecessary it seemed at the planning stage. I only regretted the trips I didn't take.*
>
> ◆
>
> *Carol Benet, Ph.D. 57, art critic, teacher, counselor, U.C. Berkeley, Belvedere, California*

➢ Eat out at a local restaurant that serves authentic food from the country you plan to visit. Chances are that the owners or staff are expatriates, and can provide valuable information.

➢ Plan your trip around a special interest such as art, history, gardening, cooking classes, biking, sailing, etc. Local organizations may be able to provide helpful information about these activities at your destination.

> ___ ⟋⟋⟍⟍ ___
>
> *I like the feeling when I'm traveling that I am responsible only for myself and my few possessions. In some ways I am in complete control of everything I do. In other ways, I have no choice but to surrender myself to the hands of the fates. The blending of these two states is romantic, enchanting, intoxicating.*
>
> ◆
>
> *Laurie Armstrong, 37, executive, Palm Springs Desert Resorts, California*

II

$\mathscr{E}$MOTIONS OF $\mathscr{D}$EPARTURE AND $\mathscr{A}$RRIVAL

Is there anything as horrible as starting on a trip?
Once you're off, that's all right, but the last moments are
earthquake and convulsion, and the feeling that you are a
snail being pulled off your rock.

—*Anne Morrow Lindbergh,* Gift From the Sea

TO PREPARE MYSELF for an upcoming trip, especially if it's to the developing world, I make a personal (and private) ritual to say good-bye to my favorite comforts and foods at home—like my soft pillow, fresh salads, and clean running water. I remind myself that these luxuries await me upon my return and that I will try to be tolerant of discomfort, unfamiliar food, and different concepts of time and personal space.

I give myself a pep talk: "Get ready, things will be different where you are traveling, don't expect to have as much control as you have at home. You can expect to be uncomfortable at times, delayed often, bored occasionally, and most certainly frustrated." Departures are

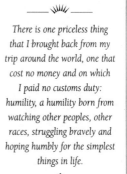

There is one priceless thing that I brought back from my trip around the world, one that cost no money and on which I paid no customs duty: humility, a humility born from watching other peoples, other races, struggling bravely and hoping humbly for the simplest things in life.

◆

Felix Marti-Ibanez,
Journey Around Myself

as easy as stepping off a curb—if you know it is there and prepare.

Even experienced travelers often forget that culture shock is sometimes most intense when you return home. You may be astonished at what you see during your travels, but it is

It is a strange thing to come home. While yet on the journey, you cannot at all realize how strange it will be.

♦

*Selma Lagerlof,
Swedish writer*

often on your return that shock settles in or has the room to make itself known to you. Take baths and walks, indulge yourself with the gift of time if you can. Let your digestive system readjust to what was once familiar food. Let your system integrate the experiences you've had.

When I returned from two years of travel, mostly in developing countries, my first trip to the supermarket was overwhelming. I just walked up and down the aisles, amazed at the choices. Immobilized by the bounty, unable to make any decisions, I left the store empty-handed. Common activities like driving a car again or listening to my friends complain about their lives were difficult to handle.

A positive way to deal with your feelings is to get involved in some volunteer activity related to your experiences overseas. The book *Bridging the Global Gap: A Handbook to Linking Citizens of the First and Third Worlds* has some great ideas. See "Volunteer Opportunities" in Chapter XVII.

TIPS

➤ To avoid feeling overwhelmed by your impending departure, allow enough time to prepare, logistically and mentally. If you are going on an extended trip,

you may need six
months or more
to prepare.

➤ You will greatly reduce
the stress associated
with your departure if
you begin packing sev-
eral days in advance.
You will then have time
to mend favorite
clothes or wash dirty
ones before packing
everything.

> *Why am I doing this? I came to
> realize that there were many
> reasons.... I believe that life is
> to be lived fully. When an
> opportunity arises...go for it.*
>
> ◆
>
> Anne Dal Vera, 42,
> resident of Frisco, Colorado
> and Amundsen-Scott
> South Pole Station

➤ Checklists can be handy for keeping track of packing,
good-byes to friends, closing up the house, canceling
the newspaper, and other things.

➤ To stay calm on the day of your departure, give
yourself plenty of time to get to the airport, train,
or bus station.

➤ If you are traveling independently, pre-book your
first night's accommodation. Chances are you'll feel
more comfortable in a new environment if you
have a plan—where
you're going (hotel,
guest-house, B&B,
youth hostel) and how
you'll get there (taxi,
public transportation,
rental car).

> *We generate fears while we sit;
> we overcome them by action.
> Fear is nature's warning signal
> to get busy.*
>
> ◆
>
> Pacific Crest Outward Bound
> School, Book of Readings

➤ When you phone or fax
the establishment of

your first night's stay, ask if they offer a free shuttle from the airport. If not, what should a taxi cost? Is there a convenient, safe local bus or subway? Can they recommend a local

A mind that is stretched by a new experience can never go back to its old dimensions.

♦

Oliver Wendell Holmes

car rental agency? (They are often less expensive than national chains.)

➢ Depending on your personality you may want to take it easy the day you arrive. Allow free time for a bath, nap, or unstructured exploration.

➢ Soon after your arrival, find a café or restaurant for what I call my "observation ritual." Sit and watch. Take specific note of the dress and behavior of women. If women don't expose their legs or arms or head, you should quickly follow suit and cover up. If they avoid eye contact, smiling, or conversations with men, be forewarned of how Western behavior may be interpreted.

➢ If you are traveling alone, or the least bit anxious about travel in the country of your choice, consider finding, upon arrival, a woman at the airport who is clearly leaving the country. Ask her specific questions such as: Is there any place that is not safe? What's the best restaurant? Is there a place where Western travelers hang out and exchange information? Are there any sights, markets or festivals you'd highly recommend?

➢ Be easy on yourself when you get back from a trip.

➢ Acclimatize slowly to your old world and make it your own again.

III

$\mathscr{S}$AFETY AND $\mathscr{S}$ECURITY

*One of the great things about travel is you find out how
many good, kind people there are.*

—*Edith Wharton*

SAFETY AND SECURITY are primary concerns for women, especially for those traveling to unfamiliar places. To travel without fear, we need to arm ourselves with knowledge, preparedness, awareness, and a flexible attitude.

We can avoid questionable neighborhoods. We can communicate that we are self-assured by walking confidently with our heads up, aware of our surroundings. When traveling alone we can avoid countries where the men are known for hassling women, such as certain Islamic countries or some areas of southern Europe. If we apply the common sense we use to survive at home, we can feel safe virtually anywhere.

The following tips are intended to increase your awareness, your comfort level, and the power you have to travel safely. One thing is certain: the more you travel the less fear you will experience. When in doubt, ask a lot of questions or ask for help.

If you are still concerned, remember this: pretend you are gutsy and that is, in fact, what you will become.

Courage is not freedom from fear; it is being afraid and going on. Once you have looked fear in the face and have overcome it, you can do it again and again and again.

♦

Pacific Crest Outward Bound School, Book of Readings

TIPS

➤ Use the common sense you've honed over the years. If you wouldn't walk in an unknown neighborhood after dark in an American city, do not do it overseas.

➤ Serendipity is at the heart of all travel. Once you are on the road, if you take small risks such as talking to a local person or accepting an invitation to someone's home, often your reward will be experiences you will long remember.

➤ Trust your instincts. Let me repeat that: TRUST YOUR INSTINCTS. Instincts are not a matter of consensus. If you feel something is off, wrong, strange—get out, move on, flee, whatever is appropriate. Do it quickly.

➤ Let your embassy or consulate know your trip itinerary if you are going somewhere unusual or potentially dangerous.

➤ Use your judgment at public demonstrations or political rallies with massive crowds. Sometimes they can become violent and should be avoided, while other times attending such gatherings can be enlightening. If you have doubts, stay near the edge of the crowd.

➤ If a group of men or young boys approaches you on the sidewalk on your side of the street, cross to the other side to give them space and you peace of mind.

➤ Scam artists such as thieves and pickpockets create distractions as a cover-up. Beware of people who may accidentally spill something on your clothing, or drop a piece of luggage in front of you. This is the time to watch your luggage and keep a hand on your valuables. Don't underestimate the skill of rip-off artists to misdirect your attention no matter how watchful you think you are.

➤ Crime in airport parking lots is increasing. Pay attention to where you park—look for parking spaces under lights, close to the terminal. Often the "off-airport" lots are safer. The shuttle bus picks you up at your car before taking you to the terminal, and drops you off at your car again. If it is dark and you feel uncomfortable, ask the driver to wait until you are safely inside your car.

➤ When you rent a car, ask for an up-to-date map and for directions to your first meeting or hotel. Be sure to ask which neighborhoods can be dangerous and should be avoided.

> ———— ⟩⟩⟩⫻ ————
>
> *Once in Old Delhi, my girlfriend and I lost our guide and thus our ride. We realized we also had no cash on us. What were we going to do, cry? No. We sat down and laughed. We wandered through dark back alleys, past men pissing in corners, until we found a fancy English bank, but they couldn't give us cash from our credit cards or travelers checks.*
>
> *An Indian executive of the bank insisted he give us enough rupees to get us to the money exchange office. The moral of the story? Don't be shy. Trust people. Ask people. Get up and go.*
>
> ◆
>
> *Lenore Thornton,*
> *Director of Financial Markets,*
> *Smith Barney, New York*

➤ When driving, if some-one yells or honks at you indicating there is something wrong, or if you are bumped, *do not stop.* Drive to a well-lit, busy place and then check it out.

Definitely take a self-defense course and never let your guard down. Then you'll feel like you can enjoy the trip.

♦

Elizabeth Harryman, 40,
radio broadcaster,
Los Angeles, California

➤ When checking into a hotel, request a room on the second to the sixth floors. Thieves target rooms on the ground level with easy escape access, and some fire hoses cannot reach above the sixth floor.

➤ If you are concerned about a lack of security in your hotel, hang out the "Do Not Disturb" sign and leave the TV on when you leave your room.

➤ Play it safe and avoid displaying your hotel room key in public, such as leaving it on your restaurant table or on the chair by the swimming pool where it could be stolen or someone could read your room number.

One thing I've learned traveling alone is to be cognizant of the hour of sunset. All over the world, towns which are filled with activity during the day can empty out once darkness descends. I never want to be the only pedestrian on the streets after dark.

♦

MBB

➤ If someone knocks on your hotel room door, verify who it is. If there is a viewport, use it. If the person identifies himself or herself as a hotel employee, request that he come back later, when you've left the room. If he insists on entering, call the front desk and confirm that someone from the staff needs to enter your room and for what purpose before letting him in.

➤ Use all locks on the hotel room doors whenever you are in the room. Consider packing a rubber door stopper. It is one of the cheapest security devices you can buy.

IV

STAYING IN TOUCH

It is difficult today to leave one's friends and family...
and yet, when it is done, I find there is a vitality to being
alone that is incredibly precious. Life rushes back into the void,
richer, more vivid, fuller than before.

—*Anne Morrow Lindbergh,* Gift From the Sea

ACCORDING TO STUDIES and polls conducted by hotel chains and travel publications, after safety, the second most important concern for women travelers is staying in touch. I agree.

Depending upon where you are going and for how long, staying in touch with home may be as simple as making a phone call, or sending a message via e-mail or fax. If you are planning a trip of a month or longer—especially in developing countries—you'll need to figure out how you will receive mail and you'll need to prepare your family and friends. Also prepare yourself to live comfortably without correspondence from home for periods of time.

If you travel to a moderately developed country, the best method to communicate easily and inexpensively with home is to send a fax. From Morocco, Ireland, or Ecuador, I could easily send and receive a one-page fax every week. This is easy

> Before I left home I asked my family to make me a tape of their favorite music. Each member contributed a piece to the tape. I have everything from Mozart to the Eagles to kids songs by Raffi. Whenever I was apprehensive, I could play the tape and feel grounded.
>
> ◆
>
> Rosemarie Enslin, 51,
> President, Enslin Associates,
> Calgary, Alberta, Canada

to do from the hotel office in most cities. When my children send a fax to me, they draw pictures and tell me all the little details of their day-to-day lives. Why do I prefer fax communication to telephones? First, you don't have to deal with time differences. Second, it is much less expensive. Third, and most important, you do not take the chance of catching a loved one in a grumpy mood (or just tired) and thus finishing the phone conversation with a sense of disappointment or anxiety. An extra emotional benefit is keeping and rereading a fax sent from home.

——— ⟨⟨⟨⟩⟩⟩ ———

When my son Mark went to Africa for the first time he was 20. We could not phone or fax each other. He was out in the bush for four months, so we could only write to each other. I pleaded with him to write to me because I would be worried about him. As part of his course work, he was required to keep a journal. He suggested: "Instead of keeping a journal, Mother, please save all my letters, they will be my journal." It was wonderful for me and I discovered my son was an insightful writer.

◆

*Lenore Thornton,
Director of Financial Markets,
Smith Barney, New York*

TIPS

➢ The easiest means of communicating with home when traveling is, without a doubt, the telephone. Now there are so many telephone company and card options that even a simple long-distance call can be complicated. Know how to use your credit card to make long distance calls before you leave on a trip and keep the access number for your long distance carrier in an easy-to-locate place in your address book.

➤ E-mail is a great way to keep in touch. If you don't travel with a computer you can sometimes get Internet access at travel agencies, hotels, or through newfound friends. Ask around.

➤ Be sure to pack a *copy* of your address book.

➤ Give a detailed itinerary to loved ones before you leave and include the fax numbers for your hotels or accommodations. Then ask your family or friends to fax you once or twice during your trip.

> _____ \\\\///_ _____
>
> *I began a tradition on my first trip overseas that I still practice today, sixteen years later: keeping a journal. I write as though I am penning a letter to my mother, complete with all the silly details I know she loves (like what kinds of pastries I've devoured and about my room's mismatched wallpaper). Re-reading my journals is like taking a trip back in time— one much more vivid than memory alone can inspire. And for a solo traveler, it gives you something to do while you're waiting for food in restaurants.*
>
> ◆
>
> *Katy Koontz, 37, freelance travel writer, Knoxville, Tennessee*

➤ If your journey is going to be unstructured and spontaneous, send postcards, faxes, or telegrams to keep people up to date as your plans develop, should there be an emergency at home.

➤ If you are going on an extended trip, find a good, organized, reliable friend to handle your correspondence. We have friends who are currently sailing around the world—taking several years to do it. Although I have their rough itinerary, they have altered their plans numerous times and I can only guess how long it will take my letters to reach them. But I can easily send a letter, fax, or postcard to the person who is in charge of their affairs. She handles all of their mail, knows where they are, more or less, and forwards mail to them.

➢ When I was traveling in remote areas without telephone service, I sent telegrams home regularly. If you keep it short, they are not expensive.

➢ You can receive mail worldwide at *poste restante*, or general delivery, at the main post office in town. Guidebooks will give you addresses. Your mail will be held for one month.

➢ I preferred to have my mail sent to the "Client Letter Service" at American Express offices in developing countries because they tend to be more reliable than post offices. Of course, you must have an American Express credit card or traveler's checks.

----- \\\\// -----

When I arrived at my hotel room in Marrakech I placed a framed picture of my daughters on the bedside table. When I returned from visiting the bustling medinas later in the day, I found fresh flowers arranged around the picture. This touching ritual continued mysteriously for two days before the maid caught me in the hall, followed me to my room, picked up my picture, kissed the photo of my girls, and through gestures told me about her own family.

◆

MBB

----- \\\\// -----

When I was traveling for two years, I took along a small tape recorder and empty cassettes. I taped letters to my parents as I traveled and sent them home every few weeks. They sent me long tapes too. I particularly loved the tapes recorded at family reunions, complete with greetings from aunts, uncles, and little cousins.

◆

MBB

American Express will provide you with a list of worldwide mailing addresses.

➤ Advise your friends and family to address your letters clearly, *printing* your name. When you go to collect mail, check under both your first and last names.

➤ Send yourself or bring home the most beautiful postcards you find. I love to display them in my office as a fond reminder of the "other me."

➤ To stay in touch with yourself, keep a journal.

———— ⚡ ————

Before you leave, consider getting involved with a ham radio club. You'll be amazed to find ham radio operators in many remote corners of the world. You'll be able to call family and friends from anywhere through a series of "patches." I was on a boat in the Sea of Cortez talking to my sister in Calgary via a kind radio operator in La Paz and another in Houston who hooked me up.

◆

Rosemarie Enslin, 51, President, Enslin Associates, Calgary, Alberta, Canada

V

HEALTH AND
HYGIENE ON THE ROAD

A journey is a person in itself; no two are alike. And all plans,
safeguards, policies, and coercion are fruitless. We find after years
of struggle that we do not take a trip; a trip takes us.

—*John Steinbeck*

WHEN I RETURN FROM AN EXOTIC PLACE, the first
thing many people ask me is, "Did you get sick?" They want
to know, specifically, if I got traveler's diarrhea. Yes, that is
my most common travel-related illness. To avoid it, be very
careful about what you drink. In countries with questionable sanitation, don't drink the water. Don't brush your
teeth with tap water, rinse your mouth in the shower, or put
ice cubes in your drinks. Drink only bottled or treated
water. Don't accept bottled water unless you see it opened
in your presence. Eat only salads and fruit that you have
prepared and peeled yourself.

Eating dairy products is a hit-or-miss affair. You
wouldn't want to pass up creamy pastries in Paris or ice
cream in Italy, but you will need to think twice before eating the same products in a developing country where refrig-
eration, sanitation, and pasteurized milk are spotty.

What about eating at food stalls? You have to take a few
chances to have some wonderful culinary encounters and
yes, even risk getting sick. In Southeast Asia some of the
best food available is found in the street stalls. You'll have
to do some investigating, though. Ask other travelers and
locals where it is safe to eat. Look for crowded places.

If you plan to travel to remote areas, take along an

emergency medical kit that can be used by health personnel. Include in it sterile syringes, needles, dressings, and gloves. I travel with my own, individually wrapped, sterile syringes. Once, after traveling for about nine months, I thought I might need another dose of gamma globulin. I was in Kathmandu at the time and although I went to a Red Cross facility, I was very pleased to hand the nurse my sterile syringe. Before my extended travels, I had asked a nurse friend to prepare an official document on her medical stationery, on which she listed all the prescription drugs, medicines, and syringes that were in my medical kit. While I never needed this document, I was prepared for a thorough border search. Preparation and precaution will help you stay healthy.

> ———— 〰️ ————
>
> *I always pack a low-fat, high-energy snack, because I get off the plane and start running (or hiking) immediately. It includes low-fat crackers, dry soup mixes, low-fat hot chocolate, carrot and celery sticks, a green apple, and always, always, a container of Grey Poupon mustard. It is great on apples. I usually carry a loaf of French bread too. If you get in late and nothing is open, you're all set. Pack an immersion coil (you can buy one at a hardware store) so you can boil water.*
>
> ♦
>
> Carole Jacobs, Travel Editor,
> Shape Magazine,
> Woodland Hills, California

TIPS

➢ Be conscious of your posture in the plane seat. A small pillow placed at the lower back helps give support. Do in-seat exercises and walk around the plane and stretch as much as possible. Be aware of posture and movement as you get up, retrieve your carry-on bag, and deplane. This is when back injuries can occur.

➤ Ever wonder why you catch a cold or the flu right after a long flight? Airlines don't introduce fresh air into the cabin as often as they used to. That means you are breathing more recycled air with everyone else's germs more often. Airborne diseases are more easy to contract. Some seasoned travelers have told me that just prior to boarding a long flight (12 hours or more) they take a broad-range antibiotic to protect themselves.

➤ Although people are always asking me how to minimize jet lag—and I have tried eating special high-protein meals and resetting my body clock before departure—I have only discovered two tips that consistently work for me. Although there is some controversy about melatonin (consult your doctor), I think it is great and use it on the plane and at my destination to help me sleep for several nights. On the plane I drink eight ounces of water every hour and avoid alcohol and coffee.

➤ Many women experience irregular menstrual cycles because of jet lag, irregular eating and sleeping, and travel-related stress. What can you do? On long flights, when periods of sitting may aggravate premenstrual edema, try walking around the plane, exercising in your seat. Also consider reducing your salt intake the week before your period. And don't become a

> _On a month-long trek in the Himalayas, the most appreciated gift I shared with fellow trekkers was the use of my sunscreen and chapstick. My lips seem to dry out and crack from the moment I step on the plane._
>
> ◆
>
> _MBB_

vegetarian overnight. If you stop eating meat, take vitamins or consume alternative sources of protein.

➤ Expect the worst menstrual period of your life and don't forget a strong cramp medicine. Take along a generous supply of tampons and panty liners.

➤ When traveling for extended periods of time and crossing many time zones, many women experience a temporary cessation of their periods. This can cause confusion about when to take birth control pills or if a pregnancy has begun. Carry the telephone number of your gynecologist back home and don't hesitate to use it if you have a problem.

➤ Avoid all but emergency gynecological examinations and treatment in developing countries. Sexually transmitted diseases can be spread by inadequately sterilized instruments.

➤ Women can safely scuba dive during menstruation. Don't believe the stories of menstrual blood attracting sharks. Most women use tampons which reduce blood loss to almost nothing.

➤ The U.S. National Park Service issues leaflets that advise women not to hike in bear country during their menstrual periods. Bears do pick up human scents, but no research has proved that black or grizzly bears are specifically attracted by menstruation odors. One study suggests that polar bears, which are more carnivorous than black or grizzly bears, show the same "maximal interest" in the scent of menstrual blood as in the scent of seals, their natural prey. Whatever the real story, use caution when camping in bear country.

➤ If you are taking oral contraceptives you may encounter problems if you contract travelers' diarrhea or an upset stomach. Your birth control pills may not be absorbed from your intestinal tract and you may be without protection. Doctors have recommended that if you vomit within three hours of taking a pill, take another one. After severe intestinal problems your birth control pills may not be effective. Always carry a backup method of contraception if you plan to be sexually active, and take along enough to last the entire trip. They are often unavailable or of poor quality in the developing world.

➤ I swear by Pepto Bismol and Alka Seltzer tablets. I recommend you pack an ample supply.

> *I always pack my running shoes, and whenever I run, I'm rewarded with a sightseeing gem. I've jogged on mountain trails in Japan, around Tiananmen Square in Beijing, through a forest in Holland, and across San Francisco's Golden Gate Bridge. I always run in the morning to catch a glimpse of how locals greet the day.*
>
> ◆
>
> *Alison Ashton, 33, Features Editor, Copley News Service, San Diego, California*

➤ If you get diarrhea, consume fluids, eat bland, dry foods, and rest. Consider short term use of Imodium, Ciprofloxacin, or seek medical assistance. Ciprofloxacin is a fabulous all-purpose antibiotic. You'll need a prescription for it, so plan ahead. It can also be used for upper respiratory problems, yeast infections, or serious traveler's diarrhea. If your symptoms don't go away after treatment with Cipro, see a doctor.

➤ Seek out the hospitals that serve the international community in major cities overseas. Call your embassy or ask the concierge at a good hotel for a reference.

➤ In hot, humid climates, yeast infections are a common travel ailment. Taking antibiotics, wearing a wet bathing suit, tight pants, shorts, or panty hose all contribute to the infection. To avoid yeast infections wear loose clothing to allow air to circulate. Cotton is better than silk or nylon. If you are prone to yeast infections, don't leave home without your medication.

➤ Long skirts with elastic waists are not only acceptable attire, they are comfortable in all types of weather. In heat, they allow air to circulate up your legs and thus reduce the incidence of yeast infections. They are also convenient when you encounter a squat toilet or when you have to go in the bushes.

➤ Be wary of swimming in fresh water in the tropics. Stagnant water can be home to snails which carry tiny larvae that cause schistosomiasis, a dangerous disease that can damage body organs. The larvae will cause your skin to itch. Drying yourself vigorously with a towel immediately after exposure may remove most of the larvae. Before wading in, ask locals about the likelihood of such snails in the water.

➤ While it may be tempting to get an inexpensive manicure, have your ears pierced, take an acupuncture treatment, or even get a tattoo, think twice about any activities that might puncture your skin, especially in developing countries.

➤ Cold water, ice, cold cream, or toothpaste will reduce severe itching. If in the wilderness, try using mud.

➤ Consider taking a travel kit of basic homeopathic remedies and a homeopathic first aid book along with your standard first aid kit. Homeopathic remedies can provide rapid, inexpensive relief from such common travel ailments as digestive problems, insect bites, rashes, sore muscles, motion sickness, and many other acute conditions.

> _Melatonin has changed my life. I no longer suffer from jet lag. On either end of the trip I take 2.5 milligrams of the sublingual melatonin for three nights. I finish all my pre-bed rituals— bath or shower, vitamins, eye mask on and ear plugs in, get into bed, lights out, and then I take the pill. It's miraculous._
>
> ♦
>
> Carol Benet, Ph.D. 57, art critic, teacher, counselor, U.C. Berkeley, Belvedere, California

➤ Pack total sunblock or a very high SPF sunscreen. It can be difficult or impossible to find high protection sunscreens many places overseas. Sun, wind, water, and snow reflection can damage many layers of skin.

➤ Take skin moisturizer, even if you think you don't need it.

➤ If you exercise regularly at home, consider jogging in the morning on your trip. Ask hotel personnel or a local person about safety and a suggestion for a scenic route. Dress modestly in loose-fitting clothes.

➤ What should be in your medical kit? See our packing list in Chapter XVII.

➤ If you are traveling to a developing country or for an extended period of time, be sure to visit your dentist prior to departure. A toothache only gets worse when the pressure decreases, like in airplanes.

➤ Drink, drink, drink, lots of bottled water to keep yourself hydrated and healthy.

➤ Wash, wash, wash, your hands. It's OK to be compulsive about this.

VI

$\mathscr{D}$INING ON THE $\mathscr{R}$OAD

Never journey without something to eat in your pocket.
If only to throw to dogs when attacked by them.

—*E. S. Bates, American writer*

MY MOST IMPORTANT TIP—pass on the road kill. Don't pass on the pastries in France, the pizza in Chicago, the *masala dosa* in India, or the food stalls in Thailand. Dining is a large part of the discovery and pleasure of travel, but it can also cause you some of your worst memories.

Some people travel specifically to eat, and one of the best ways to gain an understanding of another culture is through its cuisine. The key to dining well and staying healthy is to eat the highest quality food possible. Only you can decide how adventurous you'll be, but there is virtue in trying new things.

I may consider myself a risk taker, but when it comes to the equilibrium of my stomach, I am extremely cautious. Well, there was the time I ate bamboo grubs in northern Thailand and yak eyeballs in Tibet, but each

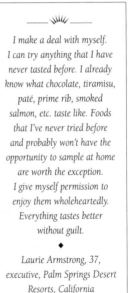

I make a deal with myself. I can try anything that I have never tasted before. I already know what chocolate, tiramisu, paté, prime rib, smoked salmon, etc. taste like. Foods that I've never tried before and probably won't have the opportunity to sample at home are worth the exception. I give myself permission to enjoy them wholeheartedly. Everything tastes better without guilt.

♦

Laurie Armstrong, 37, executive, Palm Springs Desert Resorts, California

time they were well cooked and gave me less grief than

eating a fast food hamburger in the USA. There are some gastronomic opportunities you just can't pass up!

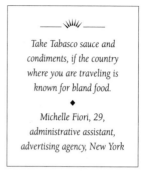

Take Tabasco sauce and condiments, if the country where you are traveling is known for bland food.

♦

Michelle Fiori, 29, administrative assistant, advertising agency, New York

After I was away from home for a few months, I craved American food and atmosphere. So in Singapore I treated myself to a lunch in an air-conditioned restaurant in an international chain hotel. The reuben sandwich was served without sauerkraut and was both disgusting and expensive, but it satisfied a need nonetheless. I lingered to write letters for hours. It was money well spent.

Bon appétit!!

TIPS

➤ Bring along a "stick to your ribs" snack for the trip. Your growling stomach may wake you up in the middle of the night in a hotel with no room service. It is lunch time for your body. My favorite snacks are granola bars and breakfast cereal, sealed in zip-lock bags.

Never trust a culture that doesn't value chocolate.

♦

Betsa Marsh, travel writer/photographer, Cincinnati, Ohio

➤ When dining at food stalls, be sure the meat is well cooked or the soup has been boiling for a while. Many of my seasoned travel friends say they wouldn't miss eating the mouth-watering local specialties available, at very reasonable prices, at food stalls. Others never go near them. As for me, I size up a stall, the clientele, the vendor, the food offered, and how it is cooked. I have had many fabulous meals and only a few painful memories from food stall experiences.

➤ Take along herbal tea. In many countries there are no decaffeinated beverages available.

➤ If you find yourself in a hole-in-the wall restaurant, where English is neither written nor spoken, just gesture to the waiter to follow you and walk right into the kitchen. Start pointing to this or that and make motions about how you want things

You'll always remember the lavish dinner at a highly-rated, upscale restaurant at your vacation destination—if for no other reason than the price. But picnics are another way to create indelible dining memories, and they stretch your travel budget at the same time. My travels have led me to memory-making picnics. On an unusually warm spring day, my husband, Jack, and I headed for the ruins of an ancient temple and theater in Sicily. There couldn't have been a more elegant setting for our simple lunch of crusty bread, salty prosciutto, cheese, sharp olives, and sparkling mineral water. Was our picnic inconsequential when compared to the breath-taking scenery? Not at all— it was a perfect complement, giving us a chance to linger and drink more deeply of the magnificent ancient theater.

◆

Marcia Schnedler,
senior travel columnist,
Universal Press Syndicate,
Little Rock, Arkansas

cooked. The staff will love it. Ham it up. It is a great way to have a terrific meal and make a friend.

➤ You'll run a lower risk of gastrointestinal ailments if you keep kosher.

➤ Be bold but don't be stupid.

———— ⸱⸱⸱⸱ ————

In eight months I managed to lose 30 pounds, even while traveling to St. Louis, San Francisco, Auckland, Melbourne, and Sydney. I had a few disasters, but mostly I faired very well. At restaurants I make the server a part of my team, confiding in him that: "I'm on a very low fat program (sounds better than 'diet') and I need your help." Then ask for exactly what you want: No COBS—No Cheese, Oil, Butter, or Sauce. The less fuss made about your food, the better.

◆

Laurie Armstrong, 37, executive, Palm Springs Desert Resorts, California

VII

ℛOMANCE AND
𝒰NWELCOME 𝒜DVANCES

It is only with the heart that one can see rightly;
what is essential is invisible to the eye.

—*Antoine de Saint-Exupery,* The Little Prince

———

ONLY YOU CAN DECIDE when or if to indulge in romance on the road. Wonderful things can happen when you meet exotic foreigners or other travelers. You could meet the love of your life, man or woman. I did and so have a few friends of mine. I met my husband (of eleven years now) in the Kathmandu Guesthouse in Nepal. But follow your instincts: the chances of an on-the-road romance continuing once you return home are not great.

At the far end of the spectrum, I had the following experience in India, when I realized that the extra Nikon zoom lens I took with me on my round-the-world journey was unnecessary. It was heavy and I rarely used it. While eating lunch in a businessman's restaurant on Connaught Circle in New Delhi, my grossly over-weight neighbor expressed great interest in my lens. He had a Nikon and had been

Journeys bring power and love back into you.

♦

Rumi,
Persian poet, Sufi mystic,
These Branching Moments

pricing similar camera equipment. He offered to buy my lens at a good price and I agreed. We set a time to meet after he finished work and had withdrawn cash from his bank.

When I met him in a populated area near the restaurant, he began acting strangely. When I asked him for the money, he whispered that I must go to bed with him first. I was enraged. Careful not to use swear words, I shouted at him, informing the crowd that he had said filthy things to me, that his mother would be

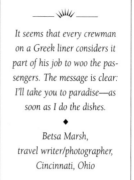

ashamed of him, that he would not go to heaven, and that he was no better than a worm. He began to sneer at me and suddenly words were not enough to express my indignation. I kicked with my sandled foot, right into his groin. He was so fat that at first it felt like kicking into jello—until my big toe reached his belt. As I doubled over in pain, he stole away. My satisfaction and his humiliation were worth my broken toe!

TIPS

➢ Be clear about what you want so you don't give mixed signals. If you want a fling, enjoy it. If you want something more lasting, examine your own feelings and ask yourself if his interest is genuine. Imagine introducing this person to friends and loved ones at home. Then trust your instincts.

➢ If you are the least bit inclined to find a lover, pack a supply of condoms. Remember, condoms bought in Bulgaria or India are not likely to be of the same quality as those bought at home. Many men, in many areas of the world, are not accustomed to discussing contraception and have negative feelings about using condoms themselves, but insist on using them nonetheless.

➤ If you are a lesbian, you are able to easily identify who is gay in your own culture. It may not be easy in other cultures. Try to learn the cultural attitudes toward gay people in the country you are visiting before you begin to flirt.

➤ In numerous countries such as Pakistan, Morocco, or India, upscale hotels and tourist offices can arrange for a reliable male escort. He acts as your guide and bodyguard. This is not a cop-out. In some Muslim areas it is worth the minimal investment to enjoy touring without continual harassment.

➤ To avoid unwanted advances, there are several things you can do:

Dress conservatively and communicate an air of confidence and respectability.

Walk with purpose.

Think and look ahead to anticipate compromising situations.

Consider wearing a wedding ring.

Try to sit or stand next to other women or family groups in restaurants, on trains or buses, or in other public places.

> ───── ⚜ ─────
>
> *If you do have a one-night fling, be careful you don't expose your money to that person. This happened to me: I got up and went to the bathroom. In the morning, after he was gone, I discovered he had stolen all the cash out of my purse. You never know who you can trust, especially if it is a guy you'll never see again.*
>
> ◆
>
> *Anonymous*

➤ If you begin to get pestered:

Completely ignore comments, cat-calls, and whistles.

Avoid all eye contact.

Don't try to speak their language.

Listen to your inner voice. If you are uncomfortable, get out of the situation immediately.

➤ If the pestering turns nasty, use forceful resistance: scream, fight, flee! Research shows that rapists often seek to feel power and control over a weaker person. Your best defense is to resist and flee.

➤ In crowded environments such as buses, men may harass you by pressing themselves against you. Don't let them get away with it. If the advance is especially ugly— suppose he presses his genitals against you— plant your elbow in his mouth, then scream at him (not swearing) in English with an air of great indignation.

A friend told me that when she goes to work out in the fitness center of her hotel, she spends all of her time in the free-weight section. Most women gravitate to the aerobics classes and the exercise machines, so she is often the only woman in an area filled with men and there is lots of good flirting.

◆

Judith Babcock Wylie, Editor,
Travelers' Tales
Love & Romance,
Santa Cruz, California

If a man begins to hassle me I always say, "I'm a very sick woman. Please do yourself a favor and leave me alone." Then I stare right past him as if I didn't hear a word he said, and walk away.

◆

Alice Boyle, 48,
advertising executive,
New York

➢ There is power in vocal embarrassment. I have found that many men are shamed by a verbal, loud woman admonishing them in public. Also shame them by shaking your finger in their faces. Even if the crowd doesn't understand your words, they will understand your indignation and gestures. Most sleazy men do not want public attention.

➢ If you want to meet people, travel with a dog.

➢ I have been told that some women meet interesting men flying First Class. I knew of a woman who, when she had a little extra cash, would buy a First Class ticket and fly short distances just to meet men.

➢ Health spa retreats, or meditation centers are good places to meet potential partners. People go to these places when they are making a life change and they are often more open and friendly. There is a time for group sharing and you talk about why you are there

---

—— ⸎ ——

If it hadn't been for my incurable wanderlust, I never would have met my husband. If it hadn't been for the gentle charms of the Caribbean, I'd probably still be single. It is a wonderful story with a moral most profound. Sometimes you have to listen to your heart and not your head. The very things that attracted me to Bill for a shipboard romance were what seemed to make him unsuitable as a permanent mate. China blue eyes, sun-blond hair, an over-all tan, and a nomadic lifestyle? Hardly the stuff on which to base anything long-term, I kept telling myself. Thankfully, Bill was smarter about relationships than I.

◆

Judy Wade, 50,
travel writer/photographer,
Phoenix, Arizona, in Travelers'
Tales: A Woman's World.

and what is going on in your life. Most people attend these sessions alone.

➤ I have noticed that women who participate in traditionally male-oriented sports (such as fishing, rock-climbing, golfing, sailing) enjoy a good deal of male companionship.

➤ If you want to meet a like-minded companion or partner, participate in an organized tour with a special focus that appeals to you, such as an archeological dig, a lesbian cruise, or an opera tour.

―――― ☼ ――――

I suggest single women who have a lot of spunk go to Alaska if they want to meet men. The average citizen is a 28-year-old male. In Alaska the saying is: "Odds are good, but the goods are odd." Personally, I didn't find the men odd.

◆

Judith Babcock Wylie, Editor,
Travelers' Tales
Love & Romance,
Santa Cruz, California

―――― ☼ ――――

My philosophy has always been: do what you love, follow your passion, and romance will follow. It has worked for me.

◆

MBB

VIII

ℬUDGET AND ℳONEY ℳATTERS

Traveling on a budget keeps you closer to the ground,
the people and the culture.

—Joe Cummings, guidebook author,
Lonely Planet Publications and Moon Publications

ALTHOUGH I HAVE BEEN ASKED dozens of times what it cost me to travel around the world for a year, it is almost impossible for me to say what it will cost *you* to travel for a month in Asia or two weeks in Europe. What you will spend depends on where you stay, where and what you eat, how you travel (plane, train, bus, rental car, on foot or bike), and how fast you travel. One person who travels twice as fast as another will spend a great deal more. Transportation, transfers in and out of cities, and lodging are a large percentage of a budget. A week lying on the beach in southern Thailand watching the waves roll in brings down your daily costs. If you stay in luxury hotels, fly

I left the States at age 21 with $600 in my pocket and a one-way ticket to New Zealand. I quickly learned how little I knew, how much there was to learn and how easy it was to travel as a woman alone—I returned from that journey 13 years later.

◆

Arlene Chester Burns, 36,
reporter for ESPN,
freelance adventurer,
photojournalist, guide,
Mosier, Oregon

everywhere, see a lot of countries in a very short trip you can spend a lot of money.

I spent under $4,000 to travel for a year, spending most of that time in Southeast Asia. That included all of my airfares, gifts, communications home— everything. Perhaps I could have spent half this amount, but I didn't want to scrimp and stay in dormitories or the cheapest hotels, always travel second class on trains, and learn to exist on rice and tea. I splurged to fly to Sri Lanka, the Maldives (where I went scuba diving...talk about expensive), and I enjoyed the old-fashioned Raj-style luxury of India's charming Maharaja Palace hotels. Remember that, most times, you will get what you pay for and many times it is worth paying a little more for the unique experience it offers.

> ───── ⚙ ─────
>
> *My well-kept secret for taking a very inexpensive getaway trip is to go somewhere, by myself or with a friend, and stay in a hostel. They have kitchens and dining rooms and common rooms. In the evenings there is a great mix of people from around the world. Most of them are under 30, but there are some "boomers" and "seniors." You basically walk into an instant dinner party, with interesting international guests.*
>
> ◆
>
> *Cathy Beaham, 36, marketing consultant, Kansas City, Missouri*

If you are traveling independently, and are not going to one location (such as a condo in Hawaii), the best way to figure out a budget for yourself is to buy a good guidebook and study it. Spend some time in a specialized travel bookstore sifting through the guides available for your destination.

Unless you have a generous budget for your travels, choose your activities and countries carefully. Many areas of Asia (Nepal, India, Indonesia, Thailand, parts of China) and South America (Peru, Ecuador) are not only inexpensive areas to travel, they are also very welcoming to women. The longer you are gone from home, the lower your per diem will be. If you have the time, plan on staying in one area for a week or more. You will meet more local people as well as experienced travelers and learn where to eat, what to do, and where to stay. When I traveled around the world I focused on remote areas where I knew I could not go on a short corporate vacation. I discovered that the longer I was gone, the less I spent.

TIPS

➤ Budget killers include: not shopping around for your plane tickets; calling home too often; using taxis excessively; eating out all the time; staying at international chain hotels. When in doubt, ask other travelers (before and during your trip) for their budget, lodging, and restaurant tips.

➤ You can save a lot of money by planning in advance. Consider alternative accommodations. For example, if you have done your research about Ireland, you will have learned about all the B&Bs in

You'll go broke if you don't do your own laundry most of the time, especially in Europe. If the radiator is running, you're in luck. Just make sure you stand by and flip the clothes often, or they'll over-cook. Use wooden hangers for drying the dark colors, or you'll end up with stains.

♦

Joan Medhurst, 49, retired professor, Alameda, California

the country. Not only are they much less expensive than staying in a hotel, they offer a huge breakfast, warm hospitality, and a chance to meet the people, not just see the sights. I have stayed in B&Bs in the USA (even in Los Angeles!) to cut costs and add charm and intimacy to my travels.

➤ Vary your travel. Try second class sometimes. Cut your transportation costs by traveling the way locals do.

➤ Ask the locals where they eat out. Leave the tourist areas of a city to find less expensive restaurants in more residential neighborhoods.

➤ Don't buy a whole new wardrobe for your trip prior to departure. Keep your pre-trip shopping to a minimum. Buy what you need as you travel.

➤ Negotiate for a hotel room? If you've got the guts, why not try? You must call the hotel directly; do not use the central 800 number. Decide how much you can spend, wait until late in the day, and speak to the hotel manager. Tell him what you can spend. Hotel rooms are a perishable item. Often they will accommodate you. Your chances of getting a lower rate for a

---

_____ ⋰⋰⋰ _____

Every year since 1979, my friend Renae and I have left husband (hers), children (hers and mine), and, most recently, our grandchildren at home for destinations overseas. This past spring, our plans were to see how inexpensively we could travel in England and Scotland and at the same time do everything that excites us: go to the theatre, see old friends, find the finest gardens, visit museums and art galleries. We wondered as well, just how flexible and adaptable we really were, how well we'd cope with the unknown. So both of us decided that nothing less than staying at youth hostels would do. On the cheap, we concurred, is not just for the young! Would we do it again? Yes!

◆

Rachel Pollack,
author, travel writer,
Denver, Colorado

room are better on the weekend in the city and during the week in the country.

➤ When making reservations for car rental, accommodations, or miscellaneous tickets, always mention your membership in an organization: AARP (American Association of Retired Persons), AAA (American Automobile Association). Often discounts are available for the asking.

➤ For airline tickets, car rentals, and hotel rooms, always ask: "Is this the lowest rate available today?"

➤ If you are staying at an establishment for a long time, or will be returning often, meet with the management and negotiate a special rate.

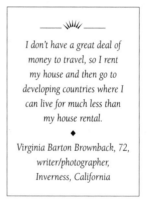

I don't have a great deal of money to travel, so I rent my house and then go to developing countries where I can live for much less than my house rental.

♦

Virginia Barton Brownback, 72, writer/photographer, Inverness, California

➤ Wait to change your money into the local currency until you arrive. Then try to change right in the airport. Take along at least $20 in small bills. These small denominations will be useful for tips and minor expenses when you don't want to break a larger traveler's check.

➤ Travel with a pocket calculator. I use it to help me figure out the exchange rate until I've worked out a simple formula. I use it to calculate the approximate amount of a credit card charge (in U.S. dollars), which I write at the bottom of the receipt.

- ➤ Make a photocopy of your credit cards, travelers checks, ATM card, passport, and eyeglass or contact lens prescription to carry in your money belt.

- ➤ Play purchasing exercises with yourself while window shopping to build your sense of the local currency, so that when you step into the store or stall you are better prepared to bargain. Memorize a currency "ladder" if you find it helps, e.g., how many *rupees* constitute $5, $10, $50? If you have a spending limit for a certain item, keep that number in mind in the foreign currency, not just in dollars.

- ➤ Protect your valuables. All of your important documents and money should be worn on your body. Buy a comfortable money belt or neck pouch. When my brother was robbed by the shoeshine boy and his buddies in Rio, they snatched the bills he took out of his trouser pocket and ran. They got $14. He had another $50 inside his sock and clothing. Only pull out small amounts of money at a time.

- ➤ Consider staying in a youth hostel. They are safe, friendly, people-oriented places filled with other budget-minded, adventurous travelers. There are over 5,000 hostels in 70 countries, including 150 in the USA. Not only does the hostel offer extensive information about what to do locally, you will meet people who have already been where you may want to go and can give you the inside scoop on the good places to see, eat, and shop. Some hostels offer bicycle, canoe, or kayak rentals. Hostels typically cost from $12 to $22 a night.

- ➤ Courier travel is neither dangerous nor illegal. Some shipping companies need to transport documents from one country to another quickly, so they ask a courier to fly to a destination with little or no checked baggage. The shipping company sends a representative to the airports of departure and arrival to handle the details of the company's checked luggage. Couriers do not fly for free—their airfare is subsidized. You must be at least 18 years old. Details in Chapter XVII.

➤ These days YMCAs aren't just for Young Christian Men! There are branches in many major cities throughout the world. You can make a reservation, with a phone call and a credit card. If you don't like the accommodations or location, you can move after the first night. Be careful that the Y is not located in an unsafe neighborhood.

------ \\|// ------

When I visited the Maldive Islands I took a boat to a secluded island. The only accommodations available were bungalows on the beach. It was an idyllic setting and I wanted to stay, but it was very expensive. I was tempted to scuba dive too, but the cost was exorbitant as well. I met privately with the manager of the resort and explained my situation—a strict budget to cover two years of traveling. I explained that I could only afford one more night, or perhaps we could work something out. Sworn to secrecy, I accepted his generous offer of a deeply discounted package that included room, board, and diving for a week. It wasn't peak season, his resort wasn't full, and he was a nice guy. Ask. You have nothing to lose.

◆

MBB

➤ What is the best way to handle your money when traveling for extended periods? If you travel in and out of major cities, use ATM withdrawals and credit card advances. If you'll be in remote areas for long periods of time, consider traveler's checks and some cash.

➤ The best exchange rate you will find is through ATMs because they provide local currency (debiting your bank account at home). They give you the wholesale exchange rate and this can be from five to ten percent higher than you get at hotels or exchange offices! Check with your bank about how to access your account overseas.

➤ Before returning to the USA, convert all of your foreign coins and bills into U.S. dollars at your airport of departure. Banks and exchange offices in the U.S. only accept bills and charge a hefty fee. Last summer I returned from Canada with ten dollars in Canadian bills. The fee to convert them to U.S. currency was five dollars.

IX

ℬARGAINING
AND 𝒯IPPING

In the act of giving something is born, and both persons involved
are grateful for the life that is born for both of them.

—*Erich Fromm,* The Art of Loving

I HATE TO SHOP AT HOME but I truly enjoy poking
through bazaars and markets looking for local handicrafts
when traveling. I use different negotiating styles with
different vendors, rickshaw drivers, or cabbies, and in
different situations. Some travelers find bargaining humili-
ating while others revel in it. It can also be an unexpected
source of local information and even friendship. But when
I find haggling with street
vendors degrading, I give
in or don't buy. I am rarely
on a budget so tight that I
can't spend an extra dollar
or two.

Once I fell in love with
a beautiful jade disk necklace in the old town in
Hanoi. I saw it in the glass
cases of several shops
before I asked the price and
began to compare the work-

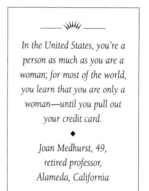

*In the United States, you're a
person as much as you are a
woman; for most of the world,
you learn that you are only a
woman—until you pull out
your credit card.*

♦

Joan Medhurst, 49,
retired professor,
Alameda, California

manship on the hand-tooled silver casing. When I finally
found a shop with several nice ones, I began to bargain.
From the very beginning, I should have realized I had met
my match, laughed, and given up. But I didn't. The

55

Vietnamese woman, about my age, grew tired of my negotiating. She appealed to my husband, to our guide, and finally, with an air of indignation after my last offer, she bellowed, "LADY YOU CHEAP!" It is a funny story to tell now but, at the time, I was humiliated. I paid her asking price and hurried off. In the end, we were both losers, because I was planning to buy three necklaces

instead of one. I smile and think of her every time I wear my "Lady You Cheap" necklace.

A friend of mine once bargained and bargained for a set of silver pony bells in a Tibetan town, but the old man offering them was absolutely unyielding in his price: $50 U.S. This seemed very high given the other goods and prices being offered at the market, and so my friend went home without the bells. Eight years later he reports that every Christmas he thinks wistfully of those bells as he puts up decorations. The moral of the story for him was to realize that the bells may well have had a history for the old man, and he was reluctant to part with them unless he got a very good price.

TIPS

➤ There is no worldwide standard for tipping for services, but my rule of thumb is: never tip less than the price of a beer in the local currency.

➤ What might be viewed as a discretionary tip in our culture may be a necessary bribe for basic services in another. For example, in India tipping is a way of getting things accomplished. I have discovered that in some countries you *must* tip restroom attendants to receive a paper towel or toilet paper. If you don't tip them, they may follow you with a stream of insults.

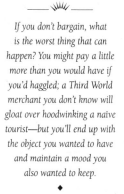

_____ ⚭ _____

If you don't bargain, what is the worst thing that can happen? You might pay a little more than you would have if you'd haggled; a Third World merchant you don't know will gloat over hoodwinking a naïve tourist—but you'll end up with the object you wanted to have and maintain a mood you also wanted to keep.

◆

Claire Walter,
editor/travel writer,
Boulder, Colorado

➤ In addition to giving a monetary tip to someone like your guide, with whom you have spent several days, add something that will be meaningful to him or her. After climbing Mt. Kilimanjaro, my husband and I tipped our guide in cash and gave him one of our day packs. He was absolutely overjoyed with it because such packs were unavailable in Tanzania.

_____ ⚭ _____

Whenever you can, give in kind instead of money. Give to an institution, or supplies to a school, or clothes to the needy, or buy them food.

◆

Olga Murray, 71, President,
Nepal Youth Opportunity
Foundation,
Sausalito, California

➤ If a taxi does not have a working meter, or the driver won't use one, avoid hassles or misunderstandings at the end of your taxi journey by negotiating the fare prior to entering the cab. Have a piece of paper available and insist he write the amount on it. Then be prepared for him to make one last effort for more money before you get out.

> In some cultures tipping is not customary or recommended. In Singapore it is officially discouraged and in Japan it is virtually unknown. In other cultures the service charge or gratuity is included in every bill. Ask a local person about the tipping customs of the country you are visiting.

> If tips are automatically included in a bill it is not necessary to leave more, but it is often customary to leave a small amount. For example, in good Parisian restaurants the French leave an additional five percent on the table.

> Be careful when you sign your credit card charge form. Most of the forms have a separate box for the gratuity. If there is no tip box on the form, ask the waiter how to include it in the charge.

Many people will ask you for money. Try to avoid giving money, especially to beggars on the street. In Third World countries, they are often professionals. Be careful whom you give to. Not only will you burn out if you are cheated, but you may turn proud people into beggars. You will often know when people really need it.

♦

Olga Murray, 71, President, Nepal Youth Opportunity Foundation, Sausalito, California

➤ Some unscrupulous restaurant personnel have been known to write the total amount of the bill, including a predetermined tip and service charge, in the top box of the charge slip. They leave the "tip" and "total" boxes empty and fill in an additional tip and new total after you have signed the bill. Ask if the tip is included and if it is, rewrite the "total" at the bottom before signing.

_____ ⟋⟋⟍⟍ _____

I remember negotiating with a boat family in Halong Bay in Vietnam who lived aboard their twelve-foot wooden skiff. They had no sewage facilities, no running water, and only a tarp to cover them in the rainy season. Two years after our encounter I still regret that I haggled over the price of fresh crab. In retrospect, I should have paid the full asking price. It wasn't much. The extra income would have made a big difference in their lives. When in doubt, pay the asking price.

◆

MBB

➤ Make sure to thank flight attendants who give you good service. They have a tough job and aren't paid well these days, nor are they allowed to accept tips. But appreciation can mean a lot.

➤ When in doubt or unsure, ask a local or a hotel employee before you are faced with a situation. If you will be traveling, conducting business, or living in a country for a long period of time, consider buying a copy of the informative *Travelers' Guide to Asian (or Latin American, or European) Customs & Manners* by Elizabeth Devine and Nancy Braganti.

✗
ℐHE ℬUSINESS ℐRAVELER

Enjoy the place you are visiting. Don't work all the time.
—*Anonymous Frequent Flyer*

———

THERE ARE TWO AREAS OF OUR LIVES in which we receive limited training: how to be a parent (not how to become one!) and how to travel efficiently (minimizing stress, maximizing safety). Business travel is an essential part of modern corporate life. After the first few trips, most individuals do not think it is "fun" or "glamorous" anymore. Is there an art to traveling smart? Frequent flyers whose jobs demand that they travel every Sunday night through Friday night will tell you yes. They live on airplanes, at airports, in hotels, driving countless miles in rental cars.

> ——— ⚜ ———
>
> *Room service? The part I love is that it's perfectly decadent. I stay in, order anything I want from room service, lounge around in my nightgown, forget my table manners, take a bath, watch trash on TV. Of course, being decadent is only enjoyable for about one night in any city.*
>
> ◆
>
> *Laurie Armstrong, 37, executive, Palm Springs Desert Resorts, California*

Even the best business travelers may not know some of these tips. Most of what I have learned has been from trial and error or from traveling with someone who is more experienced than I am.

TIPS

➤ Write down all of your confirmation numbers: hotel, car rental, flight information, etc. in your daytimer, calendar, or journal. I have jotted down these vital numbers on my airline ticket jacket, and later discovered that an efficient airline agent threw it away and gave me a clean one. If your reservation is lost or the computer is down, you will be prepared.

➤ Pack dark clothes. They don't show spots or dirt and work for most situations.

Before I pack my jewelry, whether it is expensive (or expensive-looking), I ask myself if it will fit in or if it will be appropriate in a business setting. In Paris, probably; in Quito, probably not. In some cities, wearing expensive jewelry is an invitation to mugging. Consider the context of where you are going and what you will be doing.

◆

MBB

➤ Pack everything you can into one suitcase. Then carry it aboard.

➤ If you need to be dressed in business attire at your business meeting, be sure to wear it on the plane, or carry it with you, so if your luggage is delayed or lost, you won't be forced to shop.

➤ Before driving off the lot at the rental car agency, walk around the vehicle to check for dents or other damage. Insist that everything be verified in writing by the rental agent and keep a copy.

➤ If you must leave valuables or luggage in your vehicle, be sure they are locked in the trunk or well hidden.

➤ Pack more than double the number of business cards you think you will need. Handing someone your card makes a professional statement and immediately establishes your credibility.

➤ Have your business information printed on the reverse side in the local language of the country where you will be doing business.

> *Befriend the bellboys for the most reliable information about the safety of walking from your hotel to a nearby pharmacy, restaurant, or meeting place. They are the best source of information about the neighborhood. Don't hesitate to ask them to walk you there.*
>
> ♦
>
> *Alice Boyle, 48, advertising executive, New York*

➤ If you are doing business in Asia, present your business card with both hands. After you accept your colleague's card, carefully and respectfully store it in a good place. Don't just slip it into your back pocket.

➤ Hotel alarm clocks and wake-up services can be unreliable. Pack an inexpensive sports watch with an alarm. Use the stopwatch to time international phone calls as a reminder to keep them short.

➤ The concierge at your international hotel is your best source of local information and help.

➤ How much money do you need? With a major credit card, you can obtain cash in almost every major city in the world. If you are prone to forgetting your PIN number at home, then write down a coded version in the back of your passport.

➤ Calling card thieves try to steal your long distance calling card number by looking over your shoulder in large airports, bus terminals, and train stations. Make a habit of blocking the phone buttons with your free hand or a piece of paper before you punch in your code.

➤ Laptop computers have become a major item for theft. Stay on the alert, especially when passing through security x-ray machines. A thief watches you place your laptop on the conveyer belt of the x-ray machine, then cuts in line in front of you and sets off the metal detector. While you are delayed, your laptop passes through the machine and a second thief snatches it and quickly disappears. Another technique involves someone spilling coffee or ketchup on you. When you stop and put down your bags to clean it

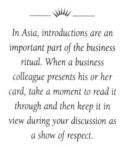

In Asia, introductions are an important part of the business ritual. When a business colleague presents his or her card, take a moment to read it through and then keep it in view during your discussion as a show of respect.

◆

Linda C. Adams, 40-plus, travel marketing consultant, Laguna Niguel, California

off, be sure your laptop is secured firmly between your legs.

➤ Should you use the hotel in-room phones or the pay phones? It depends on your budget and how many calls you plan to make. When you check in, ask what the access fee from your hotel in-room phones are. They can range from free to $1.50 per call. You may

decide to make your calls from the pay phone in
the lobby.

> If you will be making several credit card calls from
  your hotel room, don't hang up between calls, or
  you will be charged a fee for each call. Most hotel
  phone systems will allow you to hit the # key for a
  new dial tone between calls and you will avoid
  additional charges.

XI

ᴛHE
FIRST-ᴛIME
ᴛRAVELER

If I had my life to live over again, I'd try to make more
mistakes next time. I would relax. I would limber up. I would
be sillier than I have been. I would take more chances.
I would take more trips. I would climb more mountains,
swim more rivers, and watch more sunsets.

—*Nadine Stair, 85, Pacific Crest Outward Bound School,* Book of Readings

---

ALL OVER THE COUNTRY, women of all ages have asked
me to give them some words of encouragement to help
them step out the door.
Some ask, "Do you think I
should go?" I tell them yes.
To boost my self-confidence
before I took off on my solo
journey around the world,
this is what I did: every
morning as I looked into
my mirror, I asked myself,
"What's holding you back?
What is the worst that
could happen? How will
you feel about yourself in
six months or a year if you

> *I tell all young people: travel
> now while your knees are good
> and before you settle down.
> People put off travel for many
> reasons, but you should do it
> while you are mobile, active,
> interested in meeting and
> learning about people.*
>
> ◆
>
> Rosemary Gardner, 79,
> retired social worker,
> Oakland, California

don't fulfill your dream? Look at everything you have
already accomplished. This is just one more little risk. You
know that the first step is the hardest. So quit agonizing
over the decision and just go!"

TIPS

➤ Make a conscious decision about your preferred travel companion. Think through your goals and what you are willing to compromise. Do your homework. Call numerous tour operators, collect and read brochures, read guidebooks, then consider traveling with a like-minded group or alone. One of your most important decisions will be your travel companion(s). Don't make this decision hastily.

➤ If you choose to travel independently, consider arranging a homestay at the beginning of your trip. It can be as simple as renting a room with a family or as involved as an extended stay at a family guesthouse. See the Resource Section for a list of organizations that arrange homestays.

➤ Last minute purchases in the airport that make a difference: a pack of gum to relieve pressure in your ears, if needed, and for bad breath; postcards of your hometown to share or give away; snacks to stave off midnight hunger while you are adjusting to new meal times.

We all share a desire to fulfill our dreams, but few of us act on it. Over and over again women tell me that taking an adventure travel vacation was often the first time they "acted" on a totally new experience in their lives. For the first time they went somewhere alone, met new people, or learned about another culture. For the first time they experienced an active vacation and physically challenged themselves. They have all come away feeling a newfound and positive sense of self.

♦

Susan Eckert, 50, founder and president, Rainbow Adventures, Bozeman, Montana

➢ Make sure your baggage is properly routed at check-in. It is very easy for a tired airline employee to misroute a bag with the wrong destination tag. Learn the particular code for your destination.

➢ If your seat mate on an airplane, bus, or train is driving you nuts with non-stop talk, put on headphones, if you have them, smile, and turn your head away.

> _____ ⚡ _____
>
> *I couldn't get a travel agent to touch what I wanted to do (twelve countries in four months), so I organized the entire trip on the Internet. I met someone on the Web who specializes in round-the-world travel to out of the way places. In three days he had worked out all the details, at a fraction of the price I was quoted.*
>
> ◆
>
> *Preb Stritter, 72,*
> *Shelbourne Vermont*

➢ In many Third World airports you will be hassled by men in the terminal who offer cheap transportation into town. Don't accept their offers. Seek out a ground transportation desk near the baggage claim area for assistance.

➢ When you first arrive in a new city, if you can, take a half-day tour to get an overview.

➢ Before heading out to explore a new city, pick up a business card from your hotel. It's easier than you think to get lost and forget your way back, and a card in your possession will tell

> _____ ⚡ _____
>
> *Travel is learning for me. It is an open classroom. I don't go to be comfortable. I can be comfortable at home.*
>
> ◆
>
> *Virginia Barton Brownback, 72,*
> *writer/photographer,*
> *Inverness, California*

taxi drivers where you want to go. This is particularly important in countries like Thailand, Japan, or China, where you may not be able to read the script and locals may not speak or read English.

On recent trips to Turkey and British Columbia, I wore a fanny pack instead of carrying a purse. The relief I felt in never worrying "where is my purse?" was inestimable

◆

Ruth Bond, 78, retired schoolteacher, Hudson, Ohio

➤ Whether traveling by bus, train, plane, or boat, try to sit next to another woman if you want to avoid potential come-ons. You may well make a new friend.

➤ Consider leaving your purse at home and using a small fanny pack, worn around your waist, to carry bills and coins, hair brush, lipstick, and other small items. Wear it in front, not behind, which would make it a temptation to pickpockets.

➤ Also carry a small to medium backpack for all the things you'll need during the day: journal, camera, film, water bottle, sweater, guidebook. Select one with a sturdy zipper, several compartments, and padded shoulder straps. Keep the backpack locked with a combination lock.

Make a habit of turning around and looking behind you. The views and perspective can be more fantastic than those ahead.

◆

Mary Lu Abbott, editor, travel writer, Houston, Texas

———— ⚡ ————

I am one of those people who live prophylactically and sensibly and sanely. Hour after hour. Day by day. Oh, I have had my moments, and if I had it to do over again, I'd have more of them. In fact, I'd have nothing else. Just moments, one right after another, instead of living so many years ahead of each day. I have been one of those people who never go anywhere without a thermometer, a hot water bottle, a gargle, a raincoat, and a parachute. If I had it to do over again, I would go places and do things and travel lighter than I have. I would start barefoot earlier in the spring and stay that way later in the fall. I would play hooky more often. I would ride more merry-go-rounds. I'd pick more daisies. If you hold your nose to the grindstone rough and hold it down there long enough you'll soon forget there are such things as brooks that babble and a bird that sings. These things will your world compose: just you, a stone, and your darned old nose!

◆

Nadine Stair, 85,
Pacific Crest Outward Bound School, Book of Readings

XII

$\mathscr{T}$HE $\mathscr{S}$OLO $\mathscr{T}$RAVELER

> Traveling alone is not lonely; it's an extremely powerful feeling, very similar to love—it's that kind of strength. It's partly the joy of total aloneness—not loneliness—of being part of the land, as far as you can see and knowing there's nobody you need share it with.
>
> —*Christina Dodwell,* Travels with Pegasus

WHEN I STARTED TRAVELING ALONE, at age 29, it was not by choice. I couldn't find anyone to travel with me. I had only two options: stay at home and give up my dream, or go alone. So I swallowed hard, bit my lower lip, and told the world and myself that I could do it. I would do it. I would go alone. I did. And I loved it! I traveled solo for the next two years around the world.

Starting out alone does not mean staying alone. There are many other fascinating people out there traveling by themselves, just like you. At times I would hook up with a kindred spirit and we would travel together for a few days, even for

I have many opportunities to take my husband along on my travels and often do. But when I travel alone, it's an entirely different trip. Instead of being focused on the person with you, you are more observant, more attuned to every sound and detail. And you are much more likely to meet people.

♦

Kimberly Brown, 35, editor, On-line Adventure Travel magazine, Microsoft, Seattle, Washington

a month. Many of these travel companions are still close friends. My decision to go alone was one of the best choices of my life.

What's so great about it? The responses of addicted solo travelers will vary: to enjoy the freedom of making all the decisions, to experience the world unfiltered by anyone else's perspective, to live intensely, to meet people more easily and be invited into their lives more readily, to avoid a difficult travel companion, to get in touch with oneself.

Now when I create the opportunity to travel alone, it is a self-indulgent luxury. If you give it a fair chance, you too will discover that solo travel is empowering, intense, and exhilarating.

Divorce or the death of a spouse or partner can leave an avid traveler faced with the same dilemma I had. Do you choose to stay immobilized? Can you find a new travel companion? Or should you go alone? Eventually you'll begin doing day trips alone. In time you may move on to overnights, then longer journeys, until you are surprised and pleased by how confident and happy you are traveling alone.

> ───── \\||// ─────
>
> *My marriage dissolved when I was 42. That marked the first time I put on a backpack. I knew I had to begin tackling the things I was most afraid of doing alone and travel was number one on my list. I spent five weeks on the road and remember crying a lot. But I also laughed a great deal! I'm 56 at this point. I've been traveling solo all this time, except now I wouldn't have it any other way.*
>
> ◆
>
> *Evelyn Hannon, 56, editor,* Journeywoman, *Toronto, Canada*

TIPS

➤ You can *begin* traveling solo at any age. Fortunate are the women who begin traveling alone when they were young. Often they tell me they never experienced any trepidation. For those of you who aren't too sure—try it. Don't let fear stop you. Other travelers on the road and local people will support you and you'll discover how much inner strength you possess.

> Women traveling alone share similar concerns about loneliness, safety, harassment, illness, or accidents. Don't worry. Going alone is not more dangerous than traveling with a companion. Unless you are going into the back country (which you should only do with one or more companions), you will discover how fine-tuned your survival instincts are. Most countries in the world are not as violent or dangerous as our own. If you need help, ask for it.

> When you travel alone, you accept the responsibility to reach out, be extroverted, and strike up conversations with strangers. You'll find it

---

Every time we set foot on our own as solo travelers, we shave off the edge of oddness and anomaly. We are seen enjoying ourselves, taking care of ourselves. We pave the way for normalcy someday for all those women peeking out from kitchen curtains and behind veils, women who can't travel out just yet until they see that there is a road.

♦

Joan Medhurst, 49,
retired professor,
Alameda, California

I have never been frightened. And I go to places now where I would not advise younger women to go, such as certain Muslim countries. The locals laugh and giggle at me because I am alone, but they are terrific.

♦

Virginia Barton Brownback, 72,
writer/photographer,
Inverness, California

is much easier to make new friends when you are alone. You are more approachable.

➤ I am often asked, "Do you ever get lonely and what do you do about it?" I am surprised by how rarely I do get lonely. Often I fight sadness by urging myself to go to a busy sidewalk cafe and strike up a conversation. Other times I give in to my mood and become reclusive: reading, listening to music, writing in my journal or to friends and family.

➤ Recognize the difference between solitude and loneliness. I made the choice to be alone and I like my own company. Now I cherish my time alone and accept the lonely moments. They never last long. They come and go, just like at home.

_____ ⅏ _____

Everything was magnified by my being alone. In India, exploring a new city on foot, so pleasant in Europe, meant running the gauntlet: hawkers, beggars, insistent merchants came to me from everywhere, invading my personal space. With a companion, such scenes might have been merely local color. A twosome, self-contained, has its own resources. Through conversation and feedback, it can defuse the impact of the unfamiliar in a way that the solo traveler cannot. Alone and uninitiated, I felt like Snow White assaulted by Disney's animated trees. Every experience was intensely my own, undiluted by the connection to home that a familiar companion supplies. Occasionally I thought, no one on earth knows where I am. That one point held both the exhilaration and the vulnerability of traveling alone.

◆

Jo Broyles Yohay, 56, writer, New York, in Travelers' Tales: A Woman's World

➢ Use your guidebook as an indication of things to see and where to start your journey, then travel farther off the beaten path.

➢ It can be very difficult to know what is considered offensive or suggestive in segregated societies, such as in orthodox Muslim areas. At times you may feel uncomfortable or vulnerable. You may not know if the local men view you as a sex symbol, representing the immoral Western World. So take your cues from the local women. Blend in. Dress appropriately. Ask other Western women who have experience in this culture for their advice.

_____ ⋉⋊ _____

One of my most memorable encounters in Sri Lanka would not have occurred if I had not been alone and not accepted the kind offer of help from strangers. I was waiting at what I believed to be a bus stop, when a man in a battered station wagon filled with cheerful kids stopped and offered me a ride. He informed me that where I was standing was not a bus stop. I accepted his offer because of the presence of his four children. His invitation for a ride to my guesthouse led to a dinner with his wife and a school teacher, tours of the island, and a charming friendship.

♦

MBB

➢ Treat yourself to small luxuries like high tea at an elegant hotel or a manicure.

➢ When graciously offered, accept spontaneous invitations and offers of hospitality, especially from women or families. Be careful, however, not to overstay your welcome or create a hardship for the family.

➢ How do you handle eating alone in a restaurant? Choose a bistro, café, or lively place. Go prepared with reading and writing materials—postcards, letters, and your journal. Comfortably dining alone is a learned skill. Eventually you'll find yourself enjoying watching people and eavesdropping. And you won't always stay alone after being seated in a restaurant. I have often been invited to join other travelers or vice versa.

Forget groups and experts that take you on their trip. Do yourself a favor. Go alone. The anonymous single traveler, moving alone, encourages movement toward herself. She moves lightly on a springboard whose only limits are her own resources and imagination. Without a buffer to lean on, it is she who chooses: the taxi, the inn, the trail, the guide, what she wants to know, the kind of person she wants to be, how she wants to represent herself in a foreign context.

◆

Virginia Barton Brownback, 72, writer/photographer,
Inverness, California

XIII

The Older Adventurer

When your thinking becomes clouded with pessimism
and prevents you from taking risks, then you are old—
and not until then.

—*Anonymous*

———◼—▭———

IN MY GRANDMOTHER'S DAY, the only acceptable travel for a middle-aged or older woman was to visit Aunt Pearl or her grown children. Normal women in their fifties, sixties, and seventies didn't hike in New Zealand, bike in New England, join a study tour to Spain, or travel alone! Bus tours and cruise ships were the predominant form of senior travel. Society has changed. Today, as seniors stay more active and mature women are gutsier, your imagination is the limit.

Betty Ann Webster, an experienced septuagenarian traveler once told me, "I have traveled with my husband and children, with friends of many countries, with a 40-year-old son, and enjoyed all those trips, some more than others. But I do

———\\|//———

At age 60, I flew with a friend to Jasper, Alberta and we rode our bikes to Denver—1800 miles. We crossed the continental divide six times. Before we left, everyone told us not to go, that it wouldn't be safe for two women alone. In five weeks no harm came to us. One of the important things I learned was how material things can become an encumbrance and how little you need to get along. I recommend to anyone, any age, if you have a dream, you mustn't put it off five years. Everybody, please, follow your dreams.

◆

Mary Mulligan, 63, bookseller, Tattered Cover Bookstore, Denver, Colorado

like traveling alone and I've often found white hair and advanced age an advantage. For instance, I am never hassled by men as younger women traveling by themselves sometimes are. On the contrary, I'm often helped, whether I need it or not. Young Asians call me 'Aunty.' I have never encountered violence, either physical or verbal. Traveling, especially alone, involves risk, trust, judgment, and probably luck. But doesn't life itself, wherever you are?"

TIPS

➤ If you plan to travel with a group, at the time you're doing your research be sure to ask about single supplements. Several soft adventure travel companies will not charge you an extra fee if they cannot find you a roommate. (See Chapter XVII for names, addresses, and phone numbers of tour operators.)

—— \\\||// ——

A delightful side effect of developing a shock of white hair is that other travelers often feel a need to help an "older" woman. Never mind that I'm on my way to shoot the rapids of a wild New Zealand river, or explore an ancient shipwreck with a scuba partner. When I patiently listen to a teenager giving directions to a place from which I've just come, it creates a bond that invites further interaction. I've made friendships, uncovered new places, sampled exotic fare, just because for a moment I traded my need to assert self-assurance for the exhilaration of discovery.

◆

Judy Wade, 50, travel writer/photographer, Phoenix, Arizona

—— \\\||// ——

Age is no barrier to your dreams and goals.

◆

Helen Thayer, 50, skied solo to the North Pole, author of Polar Dream

- Look for special interest tours and groups or organize a journey around a special interest.

- Ask the tour company for a list of passengers who have gone on the tour you wish to take and call several of them.

- Youth hostels are not just for youth. They offer safe, clean, friendly lodging all over the world.

- Traveling by recreational vehicle is increasingly popular with many elder adventurers. Consider renting an RV to try it out. You can become a member of an RV Association and travel with other RVers, or learn RV maintenance.

- A medical emergency abroad can be quite frightening. Take out trip insurance which offers emergency evacuation.

I began traveling in my late fifties. Now, fifteen years later, I realize I have had a rich life; I have had children, romances, and gone back to school. But the excitement I have had in traveling throughout the Third World equals any of the rest. It is as exciting to me as having had babies, which was very exciting.

♦

Virginia Barton Brownback, 72, writer/photographer, Inverness, California

---

Age is not determined by the passing of years, but by our reactions to new ideas—our resistance to change. People grow old through their encasement in the past—not in their hopes for the future. Years may wrinkle the skin; but to give up faith, courage, ambition, enthusiasm for the future, and the spark of continuing growth wrinkles the soul!

♦

Pacific Crest Outward Bound School, Book of Readings

➤ Carry a list of phone numbers and addresses for U.S. embassies and consulates for the region in which you're traveling. You can contact them for emergency services. They can also help you find a reputable local doctor, dentist or hospital.

At the end of a terminal illness that was devastating to everybody, not just the victim, my husband died. I got up and shook myself and headed out. That was 25 years ago. I did a winter of ski bumming. I was 53. Then while I was in Kathmandu I saw the Peace Corps, came home and signed up. I went back to Nepal as a Peace Corps volunteer and lived in a tiny village, in a mud hut, a day's walk from the last bus stop. It was a life-changing experience. Although the Peace Corps is not easy to get into, it is the one place where there is no upper age limit.

◆

Preb Stritter, 72,
Shelbourne, Vermont

XIV
MOTHER-DAUGHTER TRAVEL

*The Earth is a book and those who do not travel
read only one page.*

—*St. Augustine*

WOMEN TRAVELING TODAY ARE DIFFERENT from the female travelers of yesterday. We are traveling more often, for pleasure and business, and more often with other women. When I mention my travels with my mother, or with my daughters, I am always amazed by the number of other women who have similar stories. More and more women are taking to the road in mother-daughter pairs. And with good reason. If you want to know about the inner life of your mother or daughters, you need almost endless opportunities to talk. The journey you take will be to the center of yourself and your relationship. The memories you will cherish for a lifetime. They will be an acknowledgment of a mother's love.

Laura and I have a wonderful time traveling together, but at times it is a challenge for me to travel "college style." Laura does not have any trouble adjusting to the luxury hotels to which I have become accustomed. The pleasure of traveling with my daughter is her openness to new adventures off the beaten path.

◆

Lenore Thornton,
*Director of Financial Markets,
Smith Barney, New York*

I was 26 when my mother and I took our first trip alone together. She left my Dad in Ohio to come visit me. I left my boyfriend in San Francisco to get to know her. We spent the weekend exploring gold mining towns in the foothills of the Sierra Nevada mountains. We talked and we laughed almost every waking moment. Quite by accident, we came upon a river rafting group preparing to ride the rapids down the Stanislaus River. Without a moment's hesitation, my mother said, "I've always wanted to do this. Let's see if we can join them!" We spent the afternoon shooting the rapids. And I spent months reflecting upon how little I knew about my responsible, school-teacher mother.

Fewer things are more rewarding so don't hesitate to do it.

TIPS

➤ If you have a congenial relationship with your mother, offer her the priceless gift of your time. Treat her to a night away—just the two of you. Plan an

---

Mama's passport photo says it all. The impish grin is brighter than the white curls, the wrinkle of smile deeper than the wrinkles of age. She's happy. She's going somewhere. With me. The mug shot proves I shouldn't have waited so long to invite her. We'd talked about a big trip we'd take "sometime," but I married and got even busier at home and work, and summers and years passed with no adventure together. Then Daddy died. Out of those sad days of winter came a sense of urgency. Time and life were galloping past, and I needed to catch up.

◆

Mary Ellen Botter,
Denver, Colorado, in Travelers'
Tales: A Woman's World

The best thing about traveling with your mom is that she can take you into the bathroom and your dad can't. And mothers don't get fed up as easily as dads.

◆

Julieclaire Sheppard, 8 years
old, Marin County, California

activity that will be very special for both of you: an elegant dinner, a play, a nice hotel, or a river rafting trip.

> For me, the best thing about traveling with my momma is sharing a bed and cuddling.
>
> ◆
>
> Annalyse Sheppard, 5 years old, Marin County, California

➤ Begin an annual tradition of taking your mother or daughter, or both, on an overnight adventure. Try camping if you enjoy the outdoors, or a resort close to home. You might choose a date near Mother's Day or her birthday.

➤ If your short excursions together are successful, consider traveling together for longer periods, even booking an organized tour—to somewhere you both have always wanted to go.

➤ If your mother is a widow, and you are single, and you usually spend the holidays together, consider exploring a new corner of the world instead of staying home. A friend of mine, a widow in her 70s, and her daughter in her 30s spend every Christmas holiday making memories— from tramping around Anasasi ruins in the Southwest to cruising in the Indonesian islands.

> I travel with my mother. I learned it's best not to share a hotel room because she's a light sleeper and likes to read and have a cup of tea at 4 a.m. She also rearranged my clothes in the closet. I let her read all the historic road signs and she lets me drive over the speed limit.
>
> ◆
>
> Virginia Sheridan, 40-plus, President, M. Silver Associates, New York

➤ If you can work it out, take your daughter on a short business trip. Visiting a metropolitan city together you can show her what your professional life is like away from home, and how you use caution to navigate safely in an unfamiliar city. You can share the places you enjoy such as museums, parks, cafés, restaurants.

➤ One of the most rewarding aspects of mothers and daughters traveling together is the way we travel. We dawdle along the road, we pause to stop and stare, to sit over a pot of tea, watching people, being quiet or talking about the idiosyncrasies of life. Be sure to plan unstructured time into your schedule.

➤ If you are traveling with your mother, ask her about her youth, her teenage years, her romances. Share some of your more private memories with her.

➤ I try to take each daughter individually on a mother/daughter outing every year. I love these trips.

_____ ⚘ _____

Traveling with my mother in Hawaii made me realize that our physical capabilities weren't at the same level anymore. We both had to learn to respect her limitations and find alternatives that we could both enjoy.

♦

Nancy Lowenherz, 33, Director of Public Relations, American Hawaii Cruises, Chicago, Illinois

_____ ⚘ _____

Mothers understand that sometimes daughters need to stop and look in or out of windows in shops, airports, cars. Girls also need primping time and mothers give it to them, even if there's a hurry to get from point A to B.

♦

Rebecca Frank, 47, Colorado Wildlife Commissioner, Grand Junction, Colorado

They give me the opportunity to focus on one child at a time and appreciate how she is growing and how our relationship is changing. There is no sibling rivalry and she has all of my attention. The sibling left at home, of course, is being spoiled rotten by her dad who is having special father/daughter time with her. It is healthy for everyone in the family. Don't wait until they're grown.

_____ ⚡ _____

The best thing about my travels with my mother is that I am always expecting to show her my world and my experiences, living in another country (Thailand), but instead we end up creating new experiences and discovering a world of our own.

◆

Laura Thornton, 25, formerly working in Thailand, now a graduate student at Princeton University and New York University

XV

$\mathscr{T}$RAVEL WITH $\mathscr{C}$HILDREN

> My father had a theory that, as the child in the womb goes
> through the various stages of the created animal world, so in
> early years it continues its progress through the primitive
> history of man: and it is therefore most necessary...
> that children should travel, at the time when in their
> epitome of history they are nomads by nature.
>
> —*Freya Stark*

BEFORE WE HAD KIDS, my husband and I were sure our style of travel wouldn't change; we would just haul our children with us—everywhere. But along with the sleepless nights, diapers, bibs, blankets, and colic, came a foreboding premonition that *I would never travel again* in any way. Although my children haven't exactly stopped me, they have slowed me down (sometimes for the better). I have learned when to take them along, when to go alone.

I am a strong advocate of numerous family vacations each year. Unfortunately, our "numerous" trips are usually short. But I feel almost any getaway is worth the hassle.

Let me clarify what I mean by family. I don't just mean the "Ozzie and Harriet" nuclear family of mom, dad, and the 2.4 children. Today's family may be any combination of children with a single parent, significant others, friends, or grandparents.

Some of the gutsiest women I know and admire are single moms who travel with their children all the time, almost everywhere. At

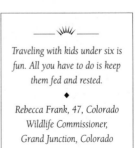

Traveling with kids under six is fun. All you have to do is keep them fed and rested.

♦

Rebecca Frank, 47, Colorado
Wildlife Commissioner,
Grand Junction, Colorado

a book signing in Fairlawn, Ohio, a single mom told me her story of driving to Alaska with her three-year-old daughter and camping for two months. I was humbled by her courage. She was still amazed and empowered by her adventure. And these stories are not unusual. I applaud every mom who has taken her children camping or traveling on her own.

Traveling with children is very different from traveling on your own, with your spouse or a friend. Although you may, as I did, have great trepidation about traveling with your children, you will soon learn that the rewards and memories are worth every inconvenience. My children have opened up new worlds for me. They have given me a different and refreshing perspective on everything we do and see. Together, we make more friends and feed off each other's energy and adventurous spirits.

> ___ \\\//_ ___
>
> *Traveling is your children's best teacher. When they observe how other people live in other places, they not only learn about the wider world but about their world too. Just don't expect them to express their thanks for the trips you've taken together. Appreciation will only come later in life.*
>
> ◆
>
> Claire Walter,
> editor/travel writer,
> Boulder, Colorado

I have simplified the basics of travel with children to five principles: PERKS.

PLANNING. Take into consideration your youngest child's interests and abilities and then work your way up the family, including yourself. Plan age-appropriate activities. Each day should include something of interest for everyone.

EVERYONE should be involved—from packing to having a say in certain activities. As soon as you know where you are going, involve your children: check out books and magazines from your library, mark up a map, discuss what distance you will travel, how long it will take to get there and what they will do during this time. After the age of four, have your children pack for themselves (once I forgot to check their bags and we arrived at our destination with 16 stuffed animals and no clean underwear or toothbrushes). Let the kids take part in the selection of the toys, games, books, and art materials you will take.

REST and relaxation should be high on your list of activities. Plan quiet time or naps. Picnics are a great way to slow down your pace. Find a park where they can run around and meet other kids while you put your feet up and read a chapter.

KEEP it simple. Under-plan your days, move at a leisurely pace, so you don't feel rushed. Traveling with children, you won't be able to see or do as much as you would without them. They need extra time to get dressed, go to the bathroom, have snacks, and work off extra energy. You can simplify your life if you locate and use the restrooms as soon as you arrive at an attraction or museum.

SNACKS and filling food are essential. If you feed them, they will be happy. At all times carry snacks they like, drinks, and stick-to-your ribs food, such as apples, bagels, or low-fat granola bars.

TIPS

➤ In a car, always buckle up your children, no matter how much they protest. A person is four times more likely to be killed and thirteen times more likely to be injured when thrown from a car.

➤ Keep your baby in the car safety seat. Stop if you have to feed or comfort your baby. A 10-pound infant in a three mph crash would be ripped from your arms with a force of 200 pounds.

➤ Safety belts are made for one person. Children should not share them.

➤ Don't use pillows or cushions to boost your child.

➤ Stop for frequent rests, exercising, and toilet breaks.

➤ Children should carry their own identification, inside their packs, in purses, or sewn into their clothing.

➤ Kids and ticks go together like peanut butter and jelly. Although most ticks are harmless, Lyme disease, caused by the bite of a rare and tiny tick, is a serious concern for every parent. Be prepared when hiking in unfamiliar areas. Prevention is not always easy. It is recommended that you and your kids wear long sleeves and long pants in the woods or grassy areas. Take a shower after being outside and check yourself and your child carefully.

➤ If you do find a tick, remove it gently but firmly with tweezers. Wear gloves and take your time. If you pull too hard or twist, you may leave the head embedded in the body. Wipe the skin with an antiseptic. *Keep the tick.* Put it in a jar to show medical authorities later if necessary. Watch for any skin reaction or any unusual symptoms and contact a physician immediately if they occur.

➤ On family vacations it seems that everyone gets a large dose of sunshine, but sunburn for a child is serious. Pack lots of sunscreen (15 SPF or greater) and use it 30 minutes before going into the sun and reapply every two hours, even if the product is touted as being waterproof. Cloudy days are just as dangerous as sunny days.

➤ Always pack a broad-brimmed hat or bonnet to protect your child's face and scalp. Keep babies out of the sun entirely.

➤ Bees love sweets, watermelon, and burgers. So do kids. What do you do when the two meet? Remove the stinger with a horizontal scraping motion using your fingernail or something flat like a driver's license. Don't squeeze or pull the stinger or you'll release more venom. Clean the site with soap and water and apply ice compresses. Make a paste of unseasoned meat tenderizer or baking soda (if you happen to have some with you) and water and apply to the area. This will neutralize the remaining venom.

➤ Your first-aid kit when traveling with kids should include tweezers (with pointed tips), bandages, gauze, fancy band-aids, antibacterial soap, adhesive tape, first aid/antibacterial cream or ointment, child and adult strength ibuprofen or aspirin, syrup of ipecac (for poison), thermometer, age-appropriate motion sickness medication, sunscreen, antihistamine for allergic reactions. A bottle of unseasoned meat tenderizer is handy for bee or wasp stings. Zip-lock bags make quick ice packs, using a hand towel for a cover.

In our family, we have a slogan: "If it is free we go and see, if you have to pay, we stay away." State parks, national forest campgrounds, and motels in small towns are bargains.

♦

Doris Scharfenberg, 71, freelance writer, grandmother of six, mother of four, Farmington Hills, Michigan

➤ When you arrive at theme parks, museums, and other crowded tourist attractions, select a central meeting place just in case you get separated from your kids. Counsel them to approach an employee to ask for help if they think they are lost. If they need to locate you in a crowd, advise them to call you by your first names. There will be lots of other mommies and daddies.

———— ⚘ ————

Traveling with children requires not only love but extra patience and ingenuity, especially ingenuity, to keep them occupied and to replace the comforting routines of home.

◆

Ruth Bond, 78,
retired schoolteacher, grandmother of four, mother of four,
Hudson, Ohio

XVI
$\mathcal{P}$ ACKING

On a long journey even a straw weighs heavy.
—*Spanish Proverb*

———

BEFORE EVERY TRIP I agonize about what to pack. Should I use my roll-aboard, a sturdy duffel bag, or a big suitcase? Which shoes, coats, clothing should I take? To reduce this stress I begin to tuck items into my bag days before departure. For a short trip, I might pack one or two days in advance. For an adventure trip, such as trekking in the Himalayas, I begin checking my gear (hiking boots, fanny pack, warm coats, flashlights, etc.) weeks before.

Recently I packed in two days for a two week trip—camping in the Sahara Desert, exploring Morocco's Atlas Mountains, Roman ruins, and imperial cities. How? The adventure travel company who operated the trip sent me a comprehensive packing list. All my gear fit into one duffel bag, and surprisingly, I didn't have to buy any new clothes or equipment.

Some women make a fetish of preparing for a trip. I'm a last-minute packer. I figure if I've got my airline ticket, passport if necessary, and a couple of credit cards, any forgotten object can always be replaced.

◆

Claire Walter,
editor/travel writer,
Boulder, Colorado

I like lists. They keep me organized. I keep several versions in my luggage and highlight in bright yellow the items I continually forget, such as dental floss, belts, and fresh batteries for flashlights. My goal is to pack so efficiently that when I unpack after a trip I discover I have worn or used every item in my bag.

TIPS

➢ Throw out the hard suitcase. It belongs to the era of the carry-on cosmetic kit. Try a roll-aboard that will fit under the seat or in the overhead. If a roll-aboard isn't for you, try a sturdy duffel bag. Shop for these in a store specializing in travel luggage.

➢ What to pack? If you are going on an organized tour, the tour company should provide you with a complete packing list tailored to your destination, its climate, and your activities. If you are traveling on your own, check out the list in Chapter XVII and begin to make it your own master list. Keep your list in a pocket of your luggage between trips. Use a colored marker to highlight the items you forget or to add to your list.

Usually you have to carry everything yourself at some point on the trip, so travel as light as possible. A good bag is one that can expand but also can be carried.

♦

Christine Wilson, 50, outdoor adventurer, guide, volunteer, Portland, Oregon

➢ How do you keep all your luggage organized? Lots of zip-lock bags! One week into your trip, you'll wish you had brought more. They keep freshly washed but not quite dry underwear separated from dry clothes, pills and vitamins separate from snacks. These see-through bags of all sizes make it easy to find everything from tampons to batteries to flashlights.

➤ Carry all your medications with you on the plane, in case your checked luggage gets lost or delayed.

> _When packing, just think— fewer shoes, more books._
>
> ◆
>
> _Elaine Petrocelli, founder and owner, Book Passage, Corte Madera, California_

➤ My list of items to take on the plane include: reading materials, ear plugs, eye mask, neck pillow, socks, a sweater, several nutritious snacks (green apple, granola bar, dried fruit), a full water bottle, chapstick, toothbrush with toothpaste, extra glasses, contact lens kit, pens, stationery, address book, and my calculator.

➤ Provide minimal information on baggage identification tags. I list only my first initial, last name and geographic area: M. Bond, San Francisco, California. If my bags are lost, airline personnel can locate me through the computer. The information I have provided is too vague for anyone to find my residence, phone number, profession, or place of employment.

> _One of the smartest things I ever did was have my colors done—not because I'm fashion-conscious, but because dressing in my "palette" allows me to pack light and still look coordinated. From one carry-on bag I can dress for just about any occasion._
>
> ◆
>
> _Glenda Winders, 50, editorial manager, Copley News Service, San Diego, California_

- ➤ Identification tags are often torn off during baggage handling. Be sure to have full identification inside your luggage.

- ➤ When I pack, I include in my carry-on bag all of my old, unread magazines and my favorite sections of the most recent Sunday *New York Times*. As I read them I discard them or give them to expatriates or other Americans who always seem to appreciate my cast-off reading materials.

- ➤ Look through your closet and select your most comfortable walking shoes for your trip. If they are almost worn out, you can leave them behind at the end of your trip. If you buy new hiking boots for a walking trip, be sure they are well broken-in and take along mole-skin for blisters just in case.

———— \\\\//// ————

I have a long necklace made of carved, wooden, children's toy animals, strung on a simple bright string. It is the only piece of jewelry I have taken on trips for a decade, and I wear it day and night when away. Invariably, it provokes curiosity, makes me seem friendlier and not so scary, and prompts people to touch the little toys, to begin to talk about these charming little carvings (in whatever language), and to finally smile. A barrier broken. All over the world, my magic necklace draws children like a magnet. Their parents follow. Even if you don't take photos, but just want to make contact, as I often do, with those beautiful people around the world who aren't found at the tourist beaches or bars, you can find something similar to provoke a smile, a moment of curiosity— an opening. And that opening is what transforms you from an outsider or an intruder into a friend.

♦

*Paula McDonald,
photojournalist,
San Ysidro, California*

➤ Pack an extra nylon duffel inside your luggage to store items in a hotel if you travel to other cities and want to leave a bag behind. It is also useful as an extra piece of luggage to carry home purchases.

➤ Pack a box of alcohol wipes. Then you can always wash your hands before meals and after pit stops.

Clothes wrinkle less in a garment bag if you hang them in the plastic covering from the dry cleaners. Plastic bags from the vegetable department of the supermarket are perfect for shoes.

♦

Laurie Armstrong, 37, executive, Palm Springs Desert Resorts, California

➤ A Swiss Army knife is an indispensable travel tool. Be sure to travel with a model that includes a pair of tweezers, scissors, a cork screw, and a toothpick. Pack it in your checked luggage.

➤ Wear layers of clothing if you are going to a place where the climate changes dramatically from day to night or if you plan lots of outdoor activities.

I never travel without a sarong. Sometimes it can be a skirt, a dress, a beach cover-up, a belt, a carry-all, a bathrobe, or a tablecloth. It is so versatile.

♦

Christine Wilson, 50, outdoor adventurer, guide, volunteer, Portland, Oregon

➤ Pack loose-fitting cotton clothing if you are going to a hot climate.

➤ Always pack your bathing suit, goggles, and cap. You never know when you'll have an opportunity to swim or hop in a hot tub, and there is no better tension reliever.

➤ Instead of packing a nightgown or pajamas I take along a large t-shirt. It doubles as a cover-up for the beach or pool and I can give it away at the end of the trip.

——— ⋇ ———

You may have to fly First or Business Class to get those soft, dark "airplane" socks to slip on when you shuck your cordovans on long flights. But it's easier to bring your own. Throw a pair of over-size hiking socks into your carry-on bag.

◆

Judy Wade, 50,
travel writer/photographer,
Phoenix, Arizona

——— ⋇ ———

The first things into my suitcase are always the bandannas—at least a half dozen per trip, in a variety of bright colors. Nothing so light, so easy to pack, has ever played so many roles, saved so many days. The simple cotton squares serve as headbands when hiking; cooling, damp necker-chiefs when worn wet in a steamy jungle; fast-drying washcloths in all those hotels and hostels that don't provide them; or washcloths in camp that can be quick-dipped in a stream and quick-dried, draped over a branch or bush. They are often the only end-of-the-day solution to "hat head" or wilted beach hair, a plague I am prone to even in the desert. Thus, my bandannas go wherever my passport goes. And, invariably, I give the lavenders and yellows and tie-dyes away along the way, coming home even lighter than I left.

◆

Paula McDonald, photojournalist, San Ysidro, California

XVII

$\mathcal{R}$ESOURCES AND $\mathcal{R}$EFERENCES

BOOKS, MAGAZINES, AND NEWSLETTERS

Reading is a great part of the pleasure of travel for me, both preparing for my adventure and reading on the trip. I look forward to having time to read when I travel. I read in the airporter bus, while I wait in airports, on flights, buses, trains, in restaurants and even, when there is no electricity, by flashlight in bed.

Anthologies and Travelogues

Aebi, Tania with Bernadette Brennan. *Maiden Voyage.* New York: Simon & Schuster, Inc., 1989. The author was an eighteen-year-old dropout from New York City when she accepted a challenge offered to her by her father: go to college or sail a twenty-six-foot sloop around the world—alone. This is the story of her voyage.

Aspen, Jean. *Arctic Daughter: A Wilderness Journey.* New York: Simon & Schuster, Inc., 1988. At twenty-two the author takes off with her husband to canoe into the Alaskan Wilderness down the Yukon to the Chadalon River into the remote Brooks Range, build a cabin, and live off the land.

Bond, Marybeth, ed. *Travelers Tales: A Woman's World.* San Francisco: Travelers' Tales, Inc., 1995. Won the gold medal of the Lowell Thomas Awards of the Society of American Travel Writers for the Best Travel Book. This eloquent collection of women's stories will move you out of your armchair, and take you along paths lined with memory, the spirit of adventure, and the strength of womanhood. Available at bookstores and mail order at 1-800-889-8969.

David-Neel, Alexandra. *My Journey to Lhasa.* North Pomfret, Vermont: Virago, 1983. The compelling story of Alexandra David-Neel, a pilgrim and an explorer in the 1920's, who in her fifty-fifth year made an exuberant journey sneaking across the forbidden border into Tibet, making her way to Lhasa disguised as a beggar man.

Davidson, Robyn. *Tracks.* New York: Random House, 1980. A high-spirited and engrossing tale of one woman's journey across Australia driven by her love of Australia's landscape, empathy for its indigenous people, and willingness to toss off her former identity.

Johnston, Tracy. *Shooting the Boh: A Woman's Voyage Down the Wildest River in Borneo.* New York: Random House, 1992. A candid account of one woman's heroic adventure down Borneo's wildest river.

Morris, Mary, and Larry O'Connor, eds. *Maiden Voyages: Writings of Women Travelers.* New York: Vintage Departures, 1993. A collection of stories, old and new, by and for women.

Morris, Mary. *Nothing to Declare: Memoirs of a Woman Traveling Alone.* New York: Houghton Mifflin Company, 1988. A travelogue and journey into the self as she relates the realities of place, poverty, and machismo of Mexico.

Murphy, Dervla. *Full Tilt: Ireland to India with a Bicycle.* New York: Overlook Press, 1965. Chronicles of Dervla's solo adventures, at age 30, through nine countries on a bicycle.

Owens, Mark and Delia. *Cry of the Kalahari.* New York: Houghton Mifflin, 1984. Carrying little more than a change of clothes and a pair of binoculars, the authors caught a plane to Africa, bought a third-hand Land Rover, and drove deep into the Kalahari desert where they lived for seven years, observing and writing about the wildlife.

Rogers, Susan Fox, ed. *Solo: On Her Own Adventure.* Seattle, Washington: Seal Press, 1996. A collection of twenty-six inspiring stories by women who describe the challenges and exhilarating rewards of going it alone.

Rogers, Susan Fox, ed. *Another Wilderness: New Outdoor Writing By Women.* Seattle, Washington: Seal Press, 1994. A compelling collection of outdoor stories by women.

Savage, Barbara. *Miles From Nowhere: A Round-the-World Bicycle Adventure.* Seattle, Washington: The Mountaineers, 1988. This is the inspiring story of Barbara Savage and her husband cycling around the world— twenty-five countries in two years.

Thayer, Helen. *Polar Dream: The Heroic Saga of the First Solo Journey by a Woman and Her Dog to the Pole.* New York: Simon & Schuster, Inc., 1993 and Bantam, Doubleday, Dell (paperback). In 1988 Helen Thayer set off to do what no other woman had done: ski to the North Pole. She was accompanied by a black husky dog named Charlie.

RESOURCE BOOKS

Benjamin, Medea and Andrea Freedman. *Bridging the Global Gap: A Handbook to Linking Citizens of the First and Third Worlds.* Carson, California: Seven Locks Press, Inc., 1989. This book discusses all the ways Americans can get involved in Third World issues. It also lists hundreds of U.S. activist organizations working on issues of alternative travel, human rights, fair trade, corporate and government responsibility, and environmental sustainability. For additional information see *The Peace Corps and More: 120 Ways to Work, Study and Travel in the Third World* by Medea Benjamin. Both books are available from Global Exchange. (See "Volunteer Opportunities" in this chapter.)

Bezruchka, Stephen. *The Pocket Doctor. Your Ticket to Good Health While Traveling.* Seattle, Washington: Mountaineers Books, 1992.

McMillon, Bill. *Volunteer Vacations: A Directory of Short Term Adventures That Will Benefit You and Others.* Chicago: Chicago Review Press, 1995. This book lists over two hundred organizations that sponsor projects worldwide in may areas, such as medical, dental, environmental, community, and executive assistance.

Schnedler, Marcia. *The Seasoned Traveler.* Castine, Maine: Cross Roads Press, 1992. A special focus on travel opportunities for people over 50.

Schroeder, Dirk. *Staying Healthy in Asia, Africa, and Latin America.* Chico, California: Moon Publications, Inc., 1993.

TRAVEL NEWSLETTERS AND MAGAZINES

Journeywoman
Quarterly women's travel magazine
50 Prince Arthur Avenue Suite 1703
Toronto, Ontario M5R 1B5 Canada
416-929-7654

Maiden Voyages
Quarterly literary magazine & guide to women's travel
109 Minna Street
Suite 240
San Francisco, CA 94105
510-528-8425

Transitions Abroad
Monthly magazine and resource guide to educational and
work opportunities abroad
Dept. TRA Box 3000
Denville, NJ 07834
800-293-0373

Travel Matters
Complimentary newsletter
Moon Publications
P. O. Box 3040
Chico, CA 95927-3040
800-345-5473

SERVICES AND ORGANIZATIONS

Tour Services Specializing in Women's Travel

Above the Clouds Trekking
P. O. Box 398E
Worcester, MA 01602
800-233-4499

Adventure Associates
*Adventure travel for women or mixed groups in the USA
and internationally*
P. O. Box 16304
Seattle, WA 98116
206-932-8352
Fax: 206-938-2654

Asia Transpacific Journeys (Boulder Adventures)
P.O. Box 1279
Boulder, CO 80306
800-642-2742

Backcountry
P.O. Box 4029
Bozeman, MT 59772
800-575-1540

Backroads
1516 5th Street
Berkeley, CA 94710-1740
800-462-2848

Becoming an Outdoors-Woman
Workshops in hunting, fishing, and camping
College of Natural Resources
University of Wisconsin, ST
Stevens Point, WI 54481-3897
715-346-2853

Call of the Wild
Women's wilderness trips in the Western USA
2519 Cedar Street
Berkeley, CA 94708
510-849-9292
Fax: 510-644-3811

Inca Floats
1311 63rd Street
Emeryville, CA 94608
510-420-1550

International Expeditions
One Environs Park
Helena, AL 35080
800-633-4734

Journeys
4011 Jackson
Ann Arbor, MI 48103
800-255-8735

Mariah Wilderness Expeditions
Women's wilderness trips in the western USA
P. O. Box 248
Point Richmond, CA 94807
415-233-2303

Mountain Travel/Sobek
6420 Fairmount Avenue
El Cerrito, CA 94530-3606
800-227-2384

Myths and Mountains
976 Tee Court
Incline Village, NV 89451
800-670-6984

Natural Habitat Adventures
2945 Center Green Court
Boulder, CO 80301
800-543-8917

Nature Expeditions International
6400 E. El Dorado Circle, Suite 210
Tucson, AZ 85715
800-869-0639

Overseas Adventure Travel
625 Mt. Auburn Street
Cambridge, MA 02138
800-221-0814

Rainbow Adventures
Adventure travel for women over 30 to destinations worldwide
15033 Kelly Canyon Road
Bozeman, MT 59715
800-804-8686
Fax: 406-587-9449

Sheri Griffith Expeditions
Women-only river rafting journeys
P. O. Box 1324
Moab, UT 84532
800-332-2439

Top Guides
1825 San Lorenzo Avenue
Berkeley, CA 94707
800-867-6777

Turtle Tours, Inc.
Box 1147/Dept. ES
Carefree, AZ 85377
602-488-3688

Wild Women Adventures
Women-only guilt-free getaways
107 N. Main Street
Sebastopol, CA 95472
800-992-1322

Wilderness Travel
801 Allston Way
Berkeley, CA 94710
800-368-2794

Womanship
Daytime sailing classes and live-aboard learning cruises
410 Severn Avenue
The Boat House
Annapolis, MD 21403
800-342-9295

The Women's Travel Club
21401 N.E. 38th Avenue
Aventura, FL 33180
800-480-4448 or 305-936-9669

Lesbian Travel

Gay and Lesbian Travel Specialists Network
2300 Market Street
Suite #142
San Francisco, CA 94114
415-552-5140

International Gay Travel Association
P. O. Box 4972
Key West, FL 33041
303-294-5135

Olivia Records and Lesbian Travel
4400 Market Street
Oakland, CA 94608
800-631-6277 or 510-655-0364

Mature/Senior Travel

Elderhostel
75 Federal Street
Boston, MA 02110
617-426-7788

Eldertreks
597 Markham Street
Toronto, Ontario, Canada M6G 2L7
800-741-7956

Folkways Institute
14600 SE Aldridge Road
Portland, OR 97236-6518
800-225-4666

Grand Circle Travel
347 Congress Street
Boston, MA 02210
800-859-0852

Overseas Adventure Travel
Worldwide adventures
625 Mt. Auburn Street
Cambridge, MA 02138
800-221-0814

Senior World Tours, Inc.
3701 Buttrick Road SE
Ada, MI 49301-9221
616-676-5885

Volunteer Opportunities

Earthwatch
Paying volunteers
680 Mount Auburn Street
Box 43
Watertown, MA 02272
617-926-8200

Global Exchange
2017 Mission Street # 303
San Francisco, CA 94110
415-255-7296

Global Volunteers
Short term volunteer opportunities for all ages
375 East Little Canada Road
St. Paul, MN 55117
800-487-1074

Habitat for Humanity
Volunteers help build homes in more than 32 countries
322 West Lamar Street
Americus, GA 31709
800-422-4828

New World Teachers
Teach English, jobs available in many countries,
no teaching experience needed
605 Market Street
Suite 800
San Francisco, CA
800-644-5424

RSVP International
Retired and senior volunteer programs in 36 countries
500 5th Avenue, 35th Floor
New York, NY 10110
212-575-1800

Worldteach
Volunteers with bachelor's degrees teach English for
one year in developing countries
Harvard Institute for International Development
1 Elliot Street
Cambridge, MA 02138-5705
617-495-5527

Homestays

American-International Homestays, Inc.
P. O. Box 7178
Boulder, CO 80306
800-876-2048

The Experiment in International Living Federation
P. O. Box 595
Putney, VT 05346
802-387-4210

Friendship Force
57 Forsyth Street, NW
Suite 900
Atlanta, GA 30303
404-522-9490

LEX Exchange, LEX America
68 Leonard Street
Belmot, MA 02178
617-489-5800

U.S. Servas
International host family organization
11 John Street
407
New York, NY 10038
212-267-0252

World Learning
P. O. Box 676
Brattleboro, VT 05302
802-257-7751

Women Welcome Women
Promotes friendship among women in more than
60 countries
c/o Joan Beyette
11215 26th Street, SW
Calgary, Alberta, Canada T2W 5C6

Courier Travel

International Association of Air Travel Couriers
Yearly registration fee: $45
P. O. Box 1349
Lake Worth, FL 33460
407-582-8320

Fear of Flying

Fearless Flyer Classes
American Airlines
1-800-451-5106

Freedom from Fear of Flying, Inc.
2021 Country Club Prado
Coral Gables, FL 33134
305-261-7042

Pegasus Fear of Flying Foundation
200 Eganfuskee Street
Jupiter, FL 33477-5068
1-800-FEAR-NOT

WORLD WIDE WEB RESOURCES

There is a lot of information about women's organizations on the Web, and to learn how to find it go to the **Travelers' Tales Web Site** (www.ora.com/ttales), scroll down to the link for Web Tours, and pull up the Women's Travel Page. Here is a sampling of what you'll find:

Accommodations
> Women's Hospitality Exchange International Network
> Internet Guide to Hostelling
> Hostels Europe
> Hostelling International
> Landfair Home Exchange

Guidebooks and Planning
> Other Travelers' Tales books
> Your Trip Abroad

Sites for Women on the Net:
> Blue Stocking
> Cybergirl
> Fabulous New Women
> FeMiNa
> Girls Internationally Writing Letters (Penpals)
> Pleiades Network: An Internet Resource For Women
> Virtual Sisterhood
> Women's Wire

Also search under Languages, Health, Currency, Transportation, Statistics, Demographics, and Security.

MISCELLANEOUS RESOURCES

Credit Card Advice

American Express: In U.S. 1-800-528-4800;
or 910-333-3211 collect from abroad.

Diner's Club: In U.S. 1-800-346-3779;
or 303-790-2433 collect from abroad.

Discover: In U.S. 1-800-347-2683
(Discover is not accepted outside the U.S.)

Mastercard: In U.S. 1-800-622-7747;
or 303-278-8000 collect from abroad.

Visa: In U.S. 1-800-336-8472;
or 410-581-7931 collect from abroad.

Traveler's Check Advice

American Express: In U.S. 1-800-221-7282. You can
also contact the American Express office nearest you.

Bank of America: In U.S. 1-800-227-6811;
or 410-581-5353 collect from abroad.

Citicorp: In U.S. 1-800-645-6556;
or 813-623-1709 collect from abroad.

Thomas Cook Mastercard: In U.S. 1-800-223-7373;
or 609-987-7300 collect from abroad.

Visa: In U.S. 1-800-227-6811 or 1-800-732-1322;
or 44-173-331-8949 collect from abroad.

$\mathscr{P}$ACKING $\mathscr{L}$IST

CLOTHING

___ belts
___ blouses
___ bras
___ boots
___ coats
___ dresses
___ gloves
___ hats
___ jackets
___ jeans
___ long t-shirt
___ panties
___ pantyhose
___ rain/sun hat
___ raincoat
___ scarves
___ shirts
___ shoes, walking
___ shoes, dress
___ shorts
___ skirts
___ slacks
___ slippers
___ socks
___ suits
___ sweaters
___ sweat suit
___ swimsuits

HYGIENE

___ body cream
___ brush/comb
___ contact lenses
      and supplies
___ dental floss
___ deodorant
___ face soap
___ foot powder
___ Kleenex
___ lip gloss
___ magnifying mirror
___ makeup
___ moleskin
___ nail brush
___ nail clippers
___ nail file
___ nail polish remover
___ razor/blades
___ shampoo/rinse
___ sunblock
___ surgical face mask
      or kerchief
___ toothbrush
___ toothpaste
___ tweezers

MEDICAL

___ prescription
medications
___ antihistamine
___ antibiotic ointment
___ antiseptic
skin cleanser
___ bandaids
___ birth control
___ cotton swabs
___ diarrhea medicine
___ insect repellent
___ motion sickness
remedy
___ muscle relaxant
___ nasal spray
___ Pepto Bismol/
Alka Seltzer
___ saline solution
___ sleeping pills
___ Sting Stop™ gel
___ thermometer
___ extra pair of
prescription glasses
(and copy of
prescription)

DOCUMENTS

___ address book
___ credit cards
___ driver's license
___ family pictures
(in plastic cover)
___ maps
___ passport/visas
___ photocopies of
passport/visas
___ passport photos
(include extras)
___ student ID card
___ travel insurance
___ travel tickets
___ travelers' checks

MISCELLANEOUS

___ alarm clock
___ batteries
___ camera/film
___ calculator
___ cash
___ clothesline
___ corkscrew
___ detergent/Woolite
___ earplugs
___ electrical converter
  & adapter plugs
___ eyeshades
___ filmshield
___ flashlight
___ games/playing cards
___ guidebooks
___ highlighter pen
  (to mark maps)
___ journal
___ luggage locks
  (combination)
___ luggage tags
___ pens/pencils
___ phrase book
___ pillowcase (doubles as
  laundry bag)
___ pocket calculator
___ reading material
___ rubber bands
___ rubber door stopper
___ safety pins
___ sewing kit

___ scissors
___ stationery
___ sunglasses
___ tape recorder
  & tapes
___ watch
___ water bottle
___ whistle
___ zip-lock bags

$\mathscr{I}$NDEX OF $\mathscr{C}$ONTRIBUTORS

About the Author

MARYBETH BOND lived in Paris for four years, Luxembourg and New Caledonia for one year. At the age of 30, fed up with a corporate job in the computer industry, she took off to travel solo for two years around the world. She has trekked across the Himalayas, the Andes, and the Alps, ridden camels across the Thar and Sahara Deserts, and elephants through the jungles of Asia. Today, she has two jobs, two kids, two mortgages, a husband, and a dog. She lives in Northern California and writes, consults for Overseas Adventure Travel, and gives keynote speeches.

Marybeth's first book, *Travelers' Tales: A Woman's World*, is an eloquent collection of women's writing that paints a rich portrait of what it means to be a woman today. *A Woman's World* won the Lowell Thomas Gold Medal for Best Travel Book from the Society of American Travel Writers Foundation. She has appeared on CNN, CNBC, America Online, and National Public Radio to share travel tips and discuss how women travel differently than men.

Whenever she can she travels—with her children, husband, girlfriends, her mother, or alone.

Notes

$\mathcal{N}$OTES

NOTES

$\mathcal{N}$OTES

TRAVELERS' TALES

OTHER TITLES IN THE SERIES

Gutsy Women is the first smaller format, "tips" book in the Travelers' Tales series. The other full-length titles in the Travelers' Tales series have a different focus. In essence, they are anthologies of the best of contemporary travel writing, organized by destination—except in special cases such as *A Woman's World*, *Food*, and *Love & Romance* (Summer '97). Each book in the award-winning Travelers' Tales series is like a hotel lobby filled with people hot from the trail, itching to tell you of their adventures, their loves, and their follies. No guidebook can take you down this experiential road the way Travelers' Tales does.

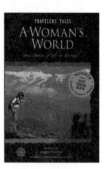

TRAVELERS' TALES A WOMAN'S WORLD

Edited by Marybeth Bond
1st Edition June 1995
ISBN 1-885211-06-6

"I loved this book! From the very first story, I had the feeling that I'd been waiting to read these women's tales for years. I also had the sense that I'd met these women before. I hadn't, of course, but as a woman and a traveler I felt an instant connection with them. What a rare pleasure."

—Kimberly Brown, *Travel & Leisure*

WINNER OF THE LOWELL THOMAS AWARD FOR BEST TRAVEL BOOK
Society of American Travel Writers

TRAVELERS' TALES BRAZIL
Edited by Annette Haddad & Scott Doggett
1st Edition January 1997, ISBN 1-885211-11-2

"Only the lowest wattage dimbulb would visit Brazil
without reading this book."
—Tim Cahill, author of *Jaguars Ripped My Flesh* and
Pecked to Death by Ducks

TRAVELERS' TALES FOOD
Edited by Richard Sterling
1st Edition November 1996, ISBN 1-885211-09-0

"Sterling's themes are nothing less than human
universality, passion and necessity, all told in stories
straight from the gut."
—Maxine Hong Kingston, author of *Woman Warrior*
and *China Men*

TRAVELERS' TALES SAN FRANCISCO
Edited by James O'Reilly,
Larry Habegger & Sean O'Reilly
1st Edition June 1996, ISBN 1-885211-08-2

"As glimpsed here through the eyes of beatniks, hippies,
surfers, 'lavender cowboys' and talented writers from all
walks, San Francisco comes to vivid, complex life."
—*Publishers Weekly*

TRAVELERS' TALES HONG KONG
Edited by James O'Reilly,
Larry Habegger & Sean O'Reilly
1st Edition January 1996, ISBN 1-885211-03-1

"*Travelers' Tales Hong Kong* will order and delight the
senses, and heighten the sensibilities, whether you are an
armchair traveler or an old China hand."
—Gladys Montgomery Jones, *Profiles Magazine*,
Continental Airlines

TRAVELERS' TALES PARIS
Edited by James O'Reilly,
Larry Habegger & Sean O'Reilly
1st Edition March 1997(est.), ISBN 1-885211-10-4

"If Paris is the main dish, here is a rich and fascinating
assortment of hors d'oeuvres. *Bon appetit et bon voyage!*"
—Peter Mayle

TRAVELERS' TALES SPAIN
Edited by Lucy McCauley
1st Edition November 1995, ISBN 1-885211-07-4

"A superb, eclectic collection that reeks wonderfully of gazpacho and paella, and resonates with sounds of heel-clicking and flamenco singing—and makes you feel that you are actually in that amazing state of mind called Iberia."
—Barnaby Conrad, author of *Matador* and *Name Dropping*

TRAVELERS' TALES FRANCE
Edited by James O'Reilly,
Larry Habegger & Sean O'Reilly
1st Edition June 1995, ISBN 1-885211-02-3

"All you always wanted to know about the French but were afraid to ask! Explore the country and its people in a unique and personal way even before getting there. Travelers' Tales: your best passport to France and the French!"
—Anne Sengés, *Journal Français d'Amérique*

TRAVELERS' TALES INDIA
Edited by James O'Reilly & Larry Habegger
1st Edition January 1995, ISBN 1-885211-01-5

"The essays are lyrical, magical and evocative: some of the images make you want to rinse your mouth out to clear the dust."
—Karen Troianello, *Yakima Herald-Republic*

TRAVELERS' TALES MEXICO
Edited by James O'Reilly & Larry Habegger
1st Edition September 1994, ISBN 1-885211-00-7

"*Travelers' Tales Mexico* opens a window on the beauties and mysteries of Mexico and the Mexicans. It's entertaining, intriguing, baffling, instructive, insightful, inspiring and hilarious—just like Mexico."
—Tom Brosnahan, co-author of Lonely Planet's *Mexico—a travel survival kit*

TRAVELERS' TALES THAILAND
Edited by James O'Reilly & Larry Habegger
1st Edition December 1993
ISBN 1-885211-05-8

"This is the best background reading I've ever seen on Thailand!"
—Carl Parkes, author of *Thailand Handbook*, *Southeast Asia Handbook* by Moon Publications

VISIT TRAVELERS' TALES
ON THE INTERNET

READ A STORY. ENTER A CONTEST. PLAN A TRIP.

Way back in 1993, we were the first travel book publisher on the World Wide Web, and our site has been growing ever since. Point your Web browser to **http://www.ora.com/ttales** and you'll discover which books we're working on, how to submit your own story, the latest writing contests you can enter, and the location of the next author event. We offer sample chapters from all of our books, as well as the occasional trip report and photo essay from our hard-working editors. Be sure to take one of our Webtours, an exhaustive list of Internet resources for each of our titles, and begin planning your own journey.

SUBMIT YOUR OWN TRAVEL TALE

Do you have a tale of your own that you would like to submit to Travelers' Tales? We highly recommend that you first read one or more of our books to get a feel for the kind of story we're looking for. For submission guidelines and a list of titles in the works, send a SASE to:

Travelers' Tales Submission Guidelines
101 Morris Street, Sebastopol, CA 95472

or send email to *ttguidelines@online.ora.com*
or check out our website at **www.ora.com/ttales**

You can send your story to the address above or via email to *ttsubmit@ora.com*. On the outside of the envelope, please indicate what country/topic your story is about. If your story is selected for one of our titles, we will contact you about rights and payment.

We hope to hear from you. In the meantime, enjoy the stories!